Ngugi wa Thiong'o
Moving the Centre
The Struggle for Cultural Freedoms

Ngugi says that *'Culture is a product of a people's history. But it also reflects that history and embodies a whole set of values by which a people view themselves and their place in time and space.'*

The West came to see itself as the centre of the universe. Cultural power, just as much as political and economic power, was controlled at the centre.

In this collection Ngugi is concerned with moving the centre in two senses – between nations and within nations – in order to contribute to the freeing of world cultures from the restrictive walls of nationalism, class, race and gender.

'The compelling emotional force of this book emerges from Ngugi's convincing emphasis on a "truly universal human culture" and his continuing ability to personalize large political issues and to persuasively politicize his own personal experiences.' – Choice

'... the poet or storyteller, he argues, cannot perform his function within his own society unless he shares and enriches its tongue. The Kenyan government only moved decisively against him when he began to do precisely that, first imprisoning him, then driving him into exile. Shifting the burden of racism and post-imperial prejudice from literature is, however, a global task, and one which Ngugi is now obliged to pursue from [New York] and in English.' – Gerald Moore in Le Monde Diplomatique

'For a long time, Ngugi's was a lone voice howling against the wind. Now people like Edward Said have joined in the war against cultural imperialism. Let battle commence.' – Anver Versi in New African

Ngugi wa Thiong'o
Decolonising the Mind
The Politics of Language in African Literature

Ngugi describes this book as 'a summary of some of the issues in which I have been passionately involved for the last twenty years of my practice in fiction, theatre, criticism and in the teaching of literature.'

'Ngugi's importance – and that of this book – lies in the courage with which he has confronted this most urgent of issues.' – Adewale Maja-Pearce in The New Statesman

Moving the Centre

The Struggle for
Cultural Freedoms

Studies in
African Literature
NEW SERIES

NGŨGĨ WA THIONG'O
Decolonising the Mind
Moving the Centre

ELDRED DUROSIMI JONES
The Writings of Wole Soyinka

SIMON GIKANDI
Reading the African Novel
Reading Chinua Achebe

EMMANUEL NGARA
Ideology & Form in African Poetry

ADEOLA JAMES (Editor)
In Their Own Voices
African women writers talk

JANE WILKINSON (Editor)
Talking with African Writers
Interviews with African poets, playwrights & novelists

MILDRED MORTIMER
Journeys through the French African Novel

KENNETH HARROW (Editor)
Faces of Islam in African Literature

EAEP Nairobi
HEINEMANN Portsmouth (N.H.)
JAMES CURREY London

Ngũgĩ
wa Thiong'o

Moving the Centre

*The Struggle for
Cultural Freedoms*

James Currey
LONDON

EAEP
NAIROBI

Heinemann
PORTSMOUTH N.H.

James Currey Ltd
54b Thornhill Square, Islington
London N1 1BE

East African Educational Publishers
PO Box 45314
Nairobi

Heinemann Educational Books Inc
361 Hanover Street
Portsmouth, New Hampshire 03801-3959

2 3 4 5 97 96 95 94

British Library Cataloguing in Publication Data

Ngũgĩ, wa Thiong'o
  Moving the Centre: The Struggle for Cultural
  Freedoms

ISBN 0–85255–530–X (James Currey Paper)
ISBN 0–85255–531–8 (James Currey Cloth)

Library of Congress Cataloging in Publication Data

Ngũgĩ wa Thiong'o, 1938—
  Moving the centre : the struggle for
  cultural freedoms / Ngũgĩ wa Thiong'o.
      p.   cm. — (Studies in African literature.
  New series)
  A collection of talks and essays, created
  between 1985 and 1990, and translated from
  Kikuyu by the author.
  1. African literature—20th century—
  History and criticism.   2. African literature
  —European influences.   I. Title.
  II. Series.
  PL8010.N485   1993
  809'.8896—dc20   92–30303
                                              CIP

ISBN 0–435–08079–2 (Heinemann)

Typeset by Colset Private Ltd
and printed in Britain by
Villiers Publications, London N6

Dedication

*To my wife
Njeeri*

Contents

Acknowledgements ix
Preface xiii

I   Freeing Culture from Eurocentrism   1

    1. Moving the Centre: Towards a Pluralism
       of Cultures   2
    2. Creating Space for a Hundred Flowers
       to Bloom: The Wealth of a Common
       Global Culture   12
    3. The Universality of Local Knowledge   25
    4. Imperialism of Language: English, a
       Language for the World?   30
    5. Cultural Dialogue for a New World   42
    6. The Cultural Factor in the Neo-colonial
       Era   47

II   Freeing Culture from Colonial Legacies   59

    7. The Writer in a Neo-colonial State   60
    8. Resistance to Damnation: The Role of
       Intellectual Workers   76
    9. The Role of the Scholar in the
       Development of African Literatures   82
  10. Post-colonial Politics and Culture   88

Contents

11. In Moi's Kenya, History is Subversive   96
12. From the Corridors of Silence: The Exile Writes Back   102
13. Imperialism and Revolution: Movements for Social Change   109

III   Freeing Culture from Racism   115

14. The Ideology of Racism: War on Peace Within and Among Nations   116
15. Racism in Literature   126
16. Her Cook, her Dog: Karen Blixen's Africa   132
17. Biggles, Mau Mau and I   136
18. Black Power in Britain   142
19. Many Years Walk to Freedom: Welcome Home Mandela!   146

IV   Matigari, Dreams and Nightmares   153

20. Life, Literature and a Longing for Home   154
21. Matigari, and the Dreams of One East Africa   159

Index   179

Acknowledgements

The original versions have been edited for this collection; occasionally they have been rewritten or enlarged. The author and the publisher wish to thank the following for permission to use the original material:

Moving the Centre: Towards a Pluralism of Cultures
The University of Leeds. Originally given as The Arthur Ravenscroft Commonwealth Literature Lecture, 4 December 1990. Also published in the *Journal of Commonwealth Literature*, Vol. 26, No. 1, 1991.

Creating Space for a Hundred Flowers to Bloom: The Wealth of a Common Culture
The University of Yale. Address, originally entitled 'The Wealth of a Common Culture' given at the conference on 'Tradition and Transition in African Letters', 19–22 April 1990. The section dealing with African Literature was first published in *The Times Literary Supplement*, December 1990.

The Universality of Local Knowledge
The Whitney Humanities Centre, Yale and the **Yale Journal of Criticism**. Originally published as a response to the main presentations by Professor Geertz and Professor Goody, Spring 1992.

Imperialism of Language: English a Language for the World?
BBC World Service and the **Yale Journal of Criticism**. This chapter was originally given as a talk with the title 'The Imperialism of

Language' in a BBC seminar on the theme 'English a Language for the World' that took place on 27 October 1988. Also published in *Yale Journal of Criticism*, Fall 1990.

The Cultural Factor in the Neo-colonial Era
Originally the keynote address at a conference on 'US Imperialism in the 1990s' held at Sheffield University in April 1988; paper given under the title 'Fighting Neo-colonialism'.

The Writer in a Neo-colonial State
Vita Books and **Black Scholar: Journal of Black Studies and Research**. Originally an address at the African Literature Association, Northwestern University, USA, 1985; published by Vita Books, June 1986, under the title 'Writing Against Neo-colonialism' and subsequently published in **Black Scholar** under the present title.

Resistance to Damnation: The Role of Intellectual Workers
UNICEF. An address to the conference, held in Harare, 1–5 March 1988, of artists, writers, musicians and intellectual workers, on the situation of children in Southern Africa, particularly in Mozambique and Angola.

The Role of the Scholar in the Development of African Literatures
Hans Zell Publishers. First published in *Research Priorities in African Literatures*, edited by Bernth Lindfors, 1984.

Post-colonial Politics and Culture
The University of Adelaide. First published in *Southern Review*, Vol. 24, No. 1, March 1991.

In Moi's Kenya, History is Subversive
Zed Books. First published as the Foreword to *Kenya's Freedom Struggle*, edited by Maina wa Kīnyattī, 1987.

From the Corridors of Silence: The Exile Writes Back
The Guardian (London). Published in *Weekend Guardian*, 21–22 October 1989, under the title 'From the Corridors of Silence'.

Imperialism and Revolution: Movements for Social Change
The Sixth International Radical, Black and Third World Book Fair.
Originally an address to the Fair in London, March 1987. It was
dedicated to Wanyiri Kihoro then in detention without trial in
Kenya for his previous activities in London as a member of the
Committee for the Release of Political Prisoners in Kenya, founded
in London in July 1982.

The Ideology of Racism: War on Peace Within and Among Nations
Liberation. Originally an address at the Racism and Peace confer-
ence, Camden Town Hall, London, 1985, given under the title
'Racism is War on Peace'.

Racism in Literature
Hackney Race Relations Unit and **Hackney Library Services**.
Originally given as a public lecture in 1984.

Her Cook, her Dog: Karen Blixen's Africa
Bogens Verden. Given as an address to the 70th anniversary of the
Danish Library Association, it was first published in *Bogens Verden*
as 'A Tremendous Service in Rectifying the Harm Done to Africa',
Copenhagen, December 1980.

Biggles, Mau Mau and I
The Guardian (London). Published in *The Guardian*, 13 August
1992 under the title 'Ngũgĩ wa Thiong'o: Ambivalent Feelings
about Biggles'.

Many Years Walk to Freedom: Welcome Home Mandela!
EMERGE. Published in April 1990, under the title 'Mandela Comes
Home'.

Life, Literature and a Longing for Home
The Guardian (London). First published as Guardian Diary, 27 May
1989.

Matigari and the Dreams of One East Africa
Geo magazine (Hamburg). First published in *Geo*, October
1989.

Acknowledgements

From the Author:

I would like to thank my publisher James Currey Ltd who first suggested the idea of bringing the new collection together. In particular, I would like to thank Keith Sambrook for his editorial input that gave the collection its present shape.

Preface

The title of this collection is taken from that of the first Arthur Ravenscroft Lecture that I gave at Leeds University on 4 December 1990. But the talks and the essays themselves are products of diverse occasions at different times and places.

The earliest piece, *Her Cook, her Dog: Karen Blixen's Africa*, was given in Copenhagen in 1981. The talk created an uproar in Denmark where Karen Blixen, alias Isaak Dinesen, was then regarded as a saint. A racist saint? I was accused of exaggerating despite the fact that I was quoting directly from her books, *Out of Africa* and *Shadows on the Grass*. The latest piece, *Post-colonial Politics and Culture*, is a transcript of a talk I gave at the University of Adelaide in September 1990 during a month's tour of Australia. It describes the continuity of Karen Blixen's Africa into post-colonial Kenya. Otherwise the majority were created between 1985 and 1990. Thus, with the sole exception of the Copenhagen piece, they fall within my years of exile from Kenya.

There are two that give me special satisfaction: *English, a Language for the World?* and *Many Years Walk to Freedom: Welcome Home Mandela!* because they are translations from the Gĩkũyũ originals. The first piece was part of a BBC seminar on English as a possible language for the world held on 27 October 1988. The translation was later broadcast on the BBC World Service. The English version, under the title *English: A Language for the World?*; and the Gĩkũyũ original, *Kĩĩngeretha: Rũthiomi rwa Thĩ Yoothe? Kaba Gĩthwaĩri!*, were first published in the 1990 Fall issue of the *Yale Journal of Criticism*. The second piece, commissioned by EMERGE, a New York based African-American news magazine, was the lead article in their March 1990 issue featuring the historic release of Nelson Mandela. But whereas the Gĩkũyũ original of the piece on language has been published in the Yale journal, the Gĩkũyũ original of the Mandela piece is still in my drawer among a good number of others. In their different destinies, the two pieces illustrate the difficulties in the way of those writing theoretical, philosophical, political and journalistic prose in an African language, moreover in conditions of exile. The Gĩkũyũ language community for instance is largely within Kenya. There are no journals or newspapers in the language inside or outside Kenya. This is true for all the other African languages in Kenya apart from the All-Kenya national language, Kiswahili. This means that those who write in African languages are confronted with a dearth of outlets for publication and therefore platforms for critical debate among those using the languages. They can only publish in translation or else borrow space from European languages journals and both options are clearly not solutions. The situation does not help much in the development of conceptual vocabulary in these languages to cope with modern technology, the sciences and the arts. The growth of writing in African languages will need a community of scholars and readers in those very languages, who will bring into the languages the wealth of literature on modern technology, arts and sciences. For this they need platforms. It is a vicious circle. So while the two pieces mirror my current involvements in the struggle to move the centre of our literary engagements from European languages to a multiplicity of locations in our languages, they also illustrate the frustrations in the way of immediate and successful realisation under the present conditions of a continent's disbelief in itself. However, difficulties in nature and life are there to be overcome. Without struggle there is no progression, said Hegel. The struggle to meet the challenge of decolonising the imagination continues and the two pieces add to my other steps in the novel, drama and children's stories, in what is clearly a long journey.

Although these talks were given and the essays written for diverse occasions at different times and places, I found that there are certain prevalent assumptions and recurring themes and concerns that unite them.

First is the assumption that for a full comprehension of the dynamics, dimensions and workings of a society, any society, the cultural aspects cannot be seen in total isolation from the economic and political ones. The quantity and quality of wealth in a community, the manner of its organisation from production to the sharing out, affect, and are affected by the way in which power is organised and distributed. These in turn affect and are affected by the values of that society as embodied and expressed in the culture of that society. The wealth and power and self-image of a community are inseparable.

The other assumption is the changing character of all societies. Nothing, not even culture, in a society can be said to have arrived at the best of all possible worlds. But since culture while being a product of the development of that society is also a repository of all the values that have been evolved by the different social strata in that society over time, in the sense that it holds a given society together it is more conservative than the economy and political life of the society which change relatively more rapidly. Culture gives that society its self-image as it sorts itself out in the economic and political fields. It therefore tends to appear as both neutral, (equally expressive of all and accessible to all) and unchanging, a stable resting place for all its members. Hence the talk of 'our values' by different societies. However, changes whether evolutionary or revolutionary can occur as result of the internal working out of the contradictions in that society in a delicate or even turbulent relationship to the external environment. In this sense society is like a human body which develops as a result of the internal working out of all its cells and other biological processes – those dying and those being born and their different combinations – and also in the external context of the air and other environmental factors. The air and food the body takes from its contact with the external environment are digested and become an integral part of the body. This is normal and healthy. But it may happen that the impact of the external factor is too strong; it is not taken in organically, in which case the body may even die. Floods, earthquakes, the wind, too much or too little air, poisoned or healthy food, overeating, overdrinking, are all external factors or activities to do with absorbing the external and they can affect the body adversely. The same with society. All societies develop under conditions of external contact with other societies at the economic, political and cultural levels. Under 'normal' circumstances, a given society is able to absorb whatever it borrows from other contacts, digest it and make it its own. But under conditions of external domination, conquest for instance, the changes are not as a result of the working out of the conflicts and tensions within, and do not arise out of the organic development of that society, but are forced upon it externally.

This may result in the society becoming deformed, changing course altogether or even dying out. Conditions of external domination and control, as much as those of internal domination and oppression, do not create the necessary climate for the cultural health of any society.

Thus, cultures that stay in total isolation from others can shrivel, dry up or wither away. Cultures under total domination from others can be crippled, deformed, or else die. Cultures that change to reflect the ever-changing dynamics of internal relations and which maintain a balanced give and take with external relations are the ones that are healthy. Hence the insistence in these essays on the suffocating and ultimately destructive character of both colonial and neo-colonial structures. A new world order that is no more than the global dominance of neo-colonial relations policed by a handful of Western nations, whether through the United Nations Security Council or not, is a disaster for the peoples of the world and their cultures. While there is a need for cultures to reach out to one another and borrow from one another this has to be on the basis of equality and mutual respect. The call for the Western-based new world order should be countered by a continued call for a new, more equitable international economic, political and cultural order within and between nations, a world order that reflects the diversity of world peoples and cultures. Hence the struggle for cultural freedoms.

Arising from all of this is the theme of moving the centre. It is this that most underlies the collection and hence the title. I am concerned with moving the centre in two senses at least. One is the need to move the centre from its assumed location in the West to a multiplicity of spheres in all the cultures of the world. The assumed location of the centre of the universe in the West is what goes by the term Eurocentrism, an assumption which developed with the domination of the world by a handful of Western nations:

> Eurocentrism [says Samir Amin in his book of the same title] is a culturalist phenomenon in the sense that it assumes the existence of

irreducibly distinct cultural invariants that shape the historical paths of different peoples. Eurocentrism is therefore anti-universalist, since it is not interested in seeking possible general laws of human evolution. But it does present itself as universalist, for it claims that imitation of the Western model by all peoples is the only solution to the challenges of our time.

Although present in all areas, economic and political and so on, the Eurocentric basis of looking at the world is particularly manifest in the field of languages, literature, cultural studies and in the general organisation of literature departments in universities in many parts of the globe. The irony is that even that which is genuinely universal in the West is imprisoned by Eurocentrism. Western civilisation itself becomes a prisoner, its jailors being its Eurocentric interpreters. But Eurocentrism is most dangerous to the self-confidence of Third World peoples when it becomes internalised in their intellectual conception of the universe.

The second sense is even more important although it is not explored extensively in these essays. Within nearly all nations today the centre is located in the dominant social stratum, a male bourgeois minority. But since many of the male bourgeois minorities in the world are still dominated by the West we are talking about the domination of the world, including the West, by a Eurocentric bourgeois, male and racial minority. Hence the need to move the centre from all minority class establishments within nations to the real creative centres among the working people in conditions of gender, racial and religious equality.

Moving the centre in the two senses – between nations and within nations – will contribute to the freeing of world cultures from the restrictive walls of nationalism, class, race and gender. In this sense I am an unrepentant universalist. For I believe that while retaining its roots in regional and national individuality, true humanism with its universal reaching out, can flower among the peoples of the earth, rooted as it is in the histories and cultures of the different peoples of the earth. Then, to paraphrase Marx, will human progress cease to resemble the pagan idol who would drink nectar but only from the skulls of the slain.

My hope is that this collection should contribute to the debate about how best to wage and win the struggle for cultural freedoms in the world. For me, moving the centre to correct the imbalances of the last four hundred years is a crucial step in that direction.

Yale
New Haven

I

*Freeing Culture
from
Eurocentrism*

1   *Moving the Centre*

Towards a Pluralism of Cultures

Sometime in 1965 I handed a piece of prose to Professor Arthur Ravenscroft in what was a class exercise in language use. It was a description of a carpenter-artist at work on wood. Later this became part of a larger evocation of life in a village in colonial Kenya between the end of the Second World War and the beginning of the Mau Mau armed struggle against British rule in 1952. When in 1966 I attended the first conference of Scandinavian and African writers in Stockholm, I presented it under the title, *Memories of Childhood*. By then it had become part of an even larger enterprise, a novel, *A Grain of Wheat*, which I wrote during my time in Leeds. The novel came out in 1967. In the copy that I signed for Arthur Ravenscroft I was happy to draw his attention to the chapter containing the exercise.

I mention the novel because in so many ways *A Grain of Wheat* symbolises, for me, the Leeds I associate with Arthur Ravenscroft's time, which was also a significant moment in the developement of African literature. This was the sixties when the centre of the universe was moving from Europe or, to put it another way, when many countries particularly in Asia and Africa were demanding and asserting their right to define themselves and their relationship to the universe from their own centres in Africa and Asia. Frantz Fanon became the prophet of the struggle to move the centre and his book, *The Wretched of the Earth*, became a kind of Bible among the African students from West and East Africa then at Leeds. In politics this moving of the centre was clear. Between 1960 and 1964, the year I came to Leeds, many countries in Africa like Tanzania, Uganda, Zaire, Nigeria, to mention only a few, had hoisted their national flags and were singing new national anthems instead of those of their conquerors from Europe as was the practice in the colonial era. Kenya had not even properly got used to its new anthem sung for the first time at the midnight of 12 December 1963. *A Grain of Wheat* celebrated the more than sixty years of Kenyan peoples' struggle to claim their own space. The political struggles to move the centre, the vast decolonisation process changing the political map of the post-war world, had also a radicalising effect in the West particularly among the young and this was best symbolised by the support the Vietnamese struggle was enjoying among the youth of the sixties. This radical tradition had in turn an impact on the African students at Leeds making them look even more critically at the content rather than the form of the decolonisation process, taking their cue from Fanon's critique in the rightly celebrated chapter in the *The Wretched of the Earth* entitled 'The Pitfalls of National Consciousness'. *A Grain of Wheat* was both a celebration of independence and a warning about those pitfalls.

In the area of culture, the struggle to move the centre was reflected in the tri-continental literature of Asia, Africa and South America. It was more dramatic in the case of Africa and the Caribbean countries where the post-war world saw a new literature in English and French consolidating itself into a tradition. This literature was celebrating the right to name the world and *A Grain of Wheat* was part of that tradition of the struggle for the right to name the world for ourselves. The new tradition was challenging the more dominant one in which Asia, Africa and South America were always being defined from the capitals of Europe by Europeans who often saw the world in colour-tinted glasses. The good and the bad African of the racist European tradition, the clowning Messrs Johnsons of the liberal European tradition or even the absence of consciousness of the colonised world in the mainstream of the European literary imagination were all being challenged by the energy of the Okonkwos of the new literature who would rather die resisting than live on bent knees in a world which they could no longer define for themselves on their terms, characters who, with their every gesture in their interaction with nature and with their social environment, were a vivid image of the fact that Africa was not a land of perpetual childhood passed over by history as it passed from East to West to find its highest expression in the Western empires of the twentieth century. Hegelian Africa was a European myth. The literature was challenging the Eurocentric basis of the vision of other worlds even when this was of writers who were not necessarily in agreement with what Europe was doing to the rest of the world. It was not a question of substituting one centre for the other. The problem arose only when people tried to use the vision from any one centre and generalise it as the universal reality.

The modern world is a product of both European imperialism and of the resistance waged against it by the African, Asian, and South American peoples. Were we to see the world through the European responses to imperialism of the likes of Rudyard Kipling, Joseph Conrad or Joyce Cary, whose work in terms of themes or location or attitude assumed the reality and experience of imperialism? Of course they responded to imperialism from a variety of ideological assumptions and attitudes. But they could never have shifted the centre of vision because they were themselves bound by the European centre of their upbringing and experience. Even where they were aware of the devastating effects of imperialism on the subject peoples, as in Conrad's description of the dying victims of colonial adventurism in *Heart of Darkness*, they could not free themselves from the Eurocentric basis of their vision.

It was actually at Makerere University College, but outside the formal structure, that I first encountered the new literatures from Africa and the Caribbean. I can still recall the excitement of reading the world from a centre other than Europe. The great tradition of European literature had invented and even defined the world view of the Calibans, the Fridays and the reclaimed Africans of their imaginations. Now the Calibans and the Fridays of the new literature were telling their story which was also my story. Even the titles, like Peter Abrahams' *Tell Freedom*, seemed to speak of a world that I knew and a hope that I shared. When Trumper, one of the characters in George Lamming's novel, *In the Castle of My Skin*, talks of his suddenly discovering his people, and therefore his world, after hearing Paul Robeson sing, 'Let My People Go', he was speaking of me and my encounter with the voices coming out of centres outside Europe. The new literatures had two important effects on me.

I wanted to write, to tell freedom, and by the time I came to Arthur Ravenscroft's class in Leeds in 1965, I had already written two novels, *The River Between* and *Weep Not Child*, a three-act play, *The Black Hermit*, two one-act plays, and nine short stories. My third novel, *A Grain of Wheat*, was to be written in Leeds but even the first two carry memories associated with Leeds. *The River Between*, the first novel to be written but the second to be published, came out in 1965 and the launch was held in Leeds with Austicks bookshop across the road flattering the author's ego with a fine display of the new book. *Weep Not Child*, the second novel but the first to be published by Heinemann in 1964, won a UNESCO First Prize in the first Black and African Writers and Artists Festival in Dakar. I heard the news while in Leeds. I got congratulations from all over the world. A UNESCO prize for literature? My financial worries in Leeds were over and I voiced my hopes to my fellow students who were not a little impressed by the fortune befalling one in their midst. You can imagine my disappointment when later I learnt that the prize was honorary after all. An honorary first prize. I have never talked about this prize or cited it as one of my accomplishments. Fortunately I heard the honorary news after I was already in the middle of my third novel, *A Grain of Wheat*, and I hoped that it would not win any honorary first prize. Not while I was a British Council Scholar in Leeds anyway.

Quite as important as my call to write was also my desire to study the new literature further. For a time, I was torn between Joseph Conrad, whom I had formally studied as a special paper in my undergraduate studies at Makerere, and George Lamming who was not known in the official curriculum at Makerere. Joseph Conrad had a certain amount of attraction. He was Polish, born in a country and a family that had known only the pleasures of domination and exile. He had learnt English late in life and yet he had chosen to write in it, a borrowed language, despite his fluency in his native tongue and in French. And what is more he had made it to the great tradition of English literature. Was he not already an image of what we, the new African writers, like the Irish writers before us, Yeats and others, could become? There was an added reason for his attraction. Conrad's most important novels were mostly located in the colonial empire: in Asia, Africa and South America. The experience of the empire was central to the sensibility in his major novels, *Lord Jim*, *Heart of Darkness*, *Victory* and *Nostromo*, not to mention all the other long and short stories set in the various outposts of the empire. Notice for instance the dominance of the images of ivory in

5

Heart of Darkness; of coal in *Victory*; of silver in *Nostromo*. *Nostromo*, in particular, was among the earliest novels to depict the coalescence of industrial and bank capital to create finance capital: what Lenin in his book *Imperialism the Highest Stage of Capitalism* once described as one of the crucial characteristics of modern imperialism. Alienation underlies most of the themes in his novels as in *Nostromo*. But Conrad had chosen to be part of the empire and the moral ambivalence in his attitude towards British imperialism stems from that chosen allegiance. George Lamming was also born in exile in the sense that his foreparents did not go to the Caribbean on a voluntary basis. The experience of the empire was also central to his novels from *In the Castle of My Skin* to *Season of Adventure*. Colonial alienation underlay all the themes in his work and he was to underwrite the centrality of the theme in his work in a book of essays under the title: *The Pleasures of Exile*. But Lamming, unlike Conrad, wrote very clearly from the other side of the empire, from the side of those who were crying out 'Let My People Go'. Conrad always made me uneasy with his inability to see any possibility of redemption arising from the energy of the oppressed. He wrote from the centre of the empire. Lamming wrote from the centre of those struggling against the empire. It seemed to me that George Lamming had more to offer and I wanted to do more work on him and on Caribbean literature as a whole.

For if the struggle to shift the base from which to view the world from its narrow base in Europe to a multiplicity of centres was reflected in the new literatures from Asia, Africa and South America, it was not similarly reflected in the critical and academic institutions in the newly independent countries, or in Europe for that matter. The study of the humanities meant literally the humanity contained in the canonised tradition of European critical and imaginative literature and, further, confined within the linguistic boundaries of each of the colonising nations. The English department at Makerere, where I went for my undergraduate studies, was probably typical of all English departments in Europe or Africa at the time. It studied English writing of the British isles from the times of Chaucer, Spenser and Shakespeare up to the twentieth century of T.S Eliot, James Joyce and Wilfred Owen. This narrowness in the study of literature based on a purely national tradition was alleviated in countries where there were other literature departments – of French, for instance. In such institutions there were competing or comparative centres in the study of humanities: the very fact that one was studying in a university where there were other literature departments meant that one was aware of other cultures. But most of these departments were largely confined to the languages of Europe and within Europe to the literature produced by the natives of that language. American literature departments were for instance completely oblivious of the poetry and fiction of the African-American peoples. In the discussion of the American novel for instance, Richard Wright, James Baldwin, Ralph Ellison were hardly mentioned as part of the central tradition of the American literary imagination. It was possible all round to graduate with a literature degree in any of the European languages without ever having heard of Achebe, Lamming, Tagore, Richard Wright, Aimé Césaire, Pablo Neruda, writers from that area of the globe that has come to be known as the Third World. In short, most universities tended to ignore the vast literatures produced, although in European languages, outside the formal boundaries of Europe and Euroamerica.

At Makerere, there was no room for this new literature (Makerere did not then have a graduate section anyway) or, from what I could gather, anywhere else at the time. Leeds came to my rescue. A Commonwealth literature conference had already been held at Leeds in 1964. Wole Soyinka one of the new voices had been a student at Leeds. Other students from Makerere, Peter Nazareth, Grant Kamenjū, Pio Zirimu were already there. There had to be something at the University of Leeds and I felt that I had to go there to get my share.

As it turned out there were no formal studies of the new literatures at Leeds. Neither the Third World literature in general nor the Commonwealth literature or even more narrowly African and Caribbean literature were then an integral part of the mainstream of the literary curricula. But there were already visiting Fellows from different parts of the world who introduced visions from centres other than Europe. There was also an openness to the voices coming out of other centres which enabled me to do research on Caribbean literature focusing on the theme of exile and identity in Caribbean literature with particular reference to the work of George Lamming. My memory of the Leeds of Arthur Ravenscroft was of an institution which was among the first to recognise and admit that there was something worthwhile out there beyond the traditional location of the European imagination even though it had used a political determinant to demarcate an area for formal admission, an area it called Commonwealth literature. The creation of a chair in Commonwealth studies, with Professor Walsh as the first occupant, and the launch of the *Journal of Commonwealth Literature* had the effect of legitimising the literature from the new centres as worthy of serious academic attention and discussion. The term 'Commonwealth literature' was woefully inadequate and African and Caribbean literature has always sat uneasily in it. African and Caribbean literature whether in English or French or Portuguese, shared a more fundamental identity and its natural literary ally was the entire literature of struggle emanating from the former colonised world of Asia, Africa and South America irrespective of linguistic barriers. But it did point out the possibility of moving the centre from its location in Europe towards a pluralism of centres, themselves being equally legitimate locations of the human imagination.

What was only tentative in the Leeds of our time, the possibility of opening out the mainstream to take in other streams, was later to become central to the debate about the relevance of literature in an African environment that raged in all the three East African universities at Nairobi, Dar es Salaam and Makerere, after most of the students who had been at Leeds at the time later returned and questioned the practices of the existing English departments. There was Grant Kamenjū in Dar es Salaam, Tanzania; Pio and Van Zirimu in Makerere, Kampala, Uganda; and I in Nairobi, Kenya. I was horrified, when I returned to Kenya in 1967, to find that the Department of English was still organised on the basis that Europe was the centre of the universe. Europe, the centre of our imagination? Ezekiel Mphahlele from South Africa, who was there before me, had fought hard to have some African texts introduced into the syllabus. Otherwise the department was still largely oblivious to the rise of the new literatures in European languages in Africa let alone the fact of the long existing tradition of African-American literature and that of Caribbean peoples. The basic question was: from what base did African peoples look at the world? Eurocentrism or Afrocentrism? The question was not that of mutual exclusion between Africa and Europe but the basis and the starting point of their interaction. I remember the excitement with which I and my two African colleagues at the University of Nairobi in the year 1968 called for the abolition of the English department as then constituted. The department was to be replaced by one which put Third World literatures, available either directly in English or through translations into English, at the centre of the syllabus without of course excluding the European tradition. Such a syllabus would emphasise the literatureness of literature rather the Englishness of that literature. The department would thus be recognising the obvious fact: that knowing oneself and one's environment was the correct basis of absorbing the world; that there could never be only one centre from which to view the world but that different people in the world had their culture and environment as the centre. The relevant question was therefore one of how one centre related to other centres. A pluralism of cultures and literatures was being assumed by the advocates of the re-named departments of literature. If the debate was initiated by the ex-students of Leeds, the actual implementation of the new structures fell to some of the professors who were there in the Leeds of the sixties. Professor Arnold Kettle in Dar es Salaam and Professor Andrew Gurr at Nairobi were instrumental in giving the new departments of literature in East Africa firm and workable structures.

It is to be noted that the mediating languages in both the new literatures from Africa and the literature departments that were accomodating them were European languages. This was a question that was to haunt me for a long time until 1977 when I started writing in Gĩkũyũ, an African language. Once again my decision finally to opt for doing all my writings mainly in Gĩkũyũ had roots in the Leeds of Arthur Ravenscroft's time. My novel, *A Grain of Wheat*, came out in 1967. Many people who have commented on my work have pointed out the obvious change in form and mood. The change in the political mood was a reflection of the intense ideological debate taking place amongst both students inside Professor Arnold Kettle's seminar on the novel and outside the formal classroom. I came to realise only too painfully that the novel in which I had so carefully painted the struggle of the Kenya peasantry against colonial oppression would never be read by them. In an interview shortly afterwards in the *Union News*, the student newspaper, in 1967, I said that I did not think that I would continue

9

writing in English: that I knew *about* whom I was writing, but *for* whom was I writing? A full discussion of the politics of language in African literature – in a sense answering that very question posed at the Leeds of the sixties – was to take place in 1987 when I published a book, *Decolonising the Mind*. But the most important thing in the immediate context is that the issue of the appropriate language for African literature had been posed at Leeds in the sixties. It was once again the question of moving the centre: from Euroepan languages to all the other languages all over Africa and the world; a move if you like towards a pluralism of languages as legitimate vehicles of the human imagination.

I believe that the question of moving towards a pluralism of cultures, literatures and languages is still important today as the world becomes increasingly one. The question posed by these new literatures whether in European or African languages is this: how were we to understand the twentieth century, or for that matter the three hundred years leading up to the twentieth century, (assuming, that is, that the study of literature is not simply a masochistic act of dwelling with the dead à la scholar Casaubon in George Eliot's *Middlemarch*)? Slavery, colonialism, and the whole web of neo-colonial relationships so well analysed by Frantz Fanon, were as much part of the emergence of the modern West as they were of modern Africa. The cultures of Africa, Asia and South America, as much as those of Europe, are an integral part of the modern world. There is no race, wrote Aimé Césaire in his famous poem, 'Return to My Native Land', which held for all time the monopoly of beauty, intelligence and knowledge; and that there was a place for all at the rendezvous of victory, human victory.

I have noted from a spell of teaching in the USA that Third World literatures tend to be treated as something outside the mainstream. Many epithets and labels ranging from 'ethnic studies' to 'minority discourses' are often used to legitimate their claims to academic attention. I am not sure of course how far Leeds has gone since the days of Arthur Ravenscroft in the sixties. But the languages and the literatures of the peoples of Africa, Asia and South America are not peripheral to the twentieth century. They are central to the mainstream of what has made the world what it is today. It is therefore not really a question of studying that which is removed from ourselves wherever we are located in the twentieth century but rather one of understanding all the voices coming from what is essentially a plurality of centres all over the world. Institutions of higher learning in Africa, Europe, Asia and America should reflect this multiplicity of cultures, literatures and languages in the ways they allocate resources for various studies. And each department of literature while maintaining its identity in the language and country of its foundation should reflect other streams, using translations as legitimate texts of study. An English or French or Spanish or Swahili student should at the same time be exposed to all the streams of human imagination flowing from all the centres in the world while retaining his or her identity as a student of English, French, Spanish or Kiswahili literature. Only in this way can we build a proper foundation for a true commonwealth of cultures and literatures.

2 Creating Space for a Hundred Flowers to Bloom

The Wealth of a Common Global Culture

Looking at the world today, one sees many countries, nations, peoples, customs, languages, and a multiplicity of apparently unsolvable conflicts and problems. But in reality the world is becoming one. Human beings who live in space circle the earth within only a few hours. They can hardly settle their eyes for long on any one country – even their own. On the earth itself, the ease of transportation has put every corner of the globe within general reach in a matter of hours, a far cry from the days of Phineas Fogg and his wager of going round the earth in eighty days.

Economic links are quite obvious. The leading financial institutions – banks, insurances, credit cards – operate in nearly all the capitals of the earth. Transnationals of all kinds link economic activities of several countries; some brands becoming almost national to many people so familiar a sight they have become in their daily lives. So a worker in Nairobi, Kenya in an automobile warehouse can have the same employer as many others in North, Central, South American and Asian cities. Messrs Coca-Cola and MacDonalds, between themselves, are making the world in their own image. It is of course true that these processes are controlled by a handful of Western transnationals. IMF and the World Bank dictate the social and economic policies of many countries. But it does mean that many workers, many nations, even when they may not be consciously aware of it, are linked to the same controlling central forces. Their apparently individual struggles against any excesses of the central command are invisibly linked to others. Workers for instance could be struggling against the same employer even though they are located in the different capitals and nations of the earth. As for the distribution of power, a handful of Western nations still dominate various other nations. Hence the experiences of national liberation and even the internal social struggles of many nations might be shaped in a similar way by the fact of their being aimed against the practices of a common enemy.

Those global economic and political processes invariably give rise to cultural links. The evolution of the present global order over the last five hundred years has seen the world being dominated by a handful of languages; European languages of course and the cultures these have carried will have shaped the dominated in similar ways. The fax, the telex, the computer, while facilitating communications, also mean the instant spread of information and culture across national boundaries. Television images via satellites enable the whole world to experience the Palestinian uprising in the Middle East, the struggle for Amandla in South Africa, the mass uprisings and calls for democratic accountability to the people in Eastern Europe, at about the same time. Mandela could speak to billions in the world from his platform at the Wembley stadium in London, the concert in his honour there becoming part of a global instant experience. His release from 27 years in prison was watched by millions. Words like perestroika, glasnost, amandla, a luta continua, people power, democracy, socialism have become part of a common vocabulary.

In terms of the structures of domination, subordination and resistance, a common global experience is emerging. Gradually a vocabulary of concepts of domination and revolt become part of a shared intellectual tradition.

Literature, more than all the fleeting images brought about by the screen or newsprint, is one of the more enduring multinational cultural processes which have been building the basis of a shared common tradition. From the ancient and modern literatures names of characters like Rama, Sinbad, Ali Baba, Isis and Osiris, Abunuwasi, Anansi, Hercules, Odysseus, Achilles, Helen, Oedipus, Prometheus, Gargantua and Pantagruel, Faustus, Hamlet, Okonkwo, to mention just a few; and writers like Aeschylus, Shakespeare, Pushkin, Dostoevsky, Tolstoy, Goethe, Schiller, Thomas Mann, Brecht, Richard Wright, Alice Walker, Faulkner, Melville, Lu Hsun, Kim Chi Ha, the Grimm brothers, Andersen, Chinua Achebe, Wole Soyinka, Alex la Guma, Sembene Ousmane,

13

have become part of a global inheritance.

Inevitably because of the position of domination of Europe *vis-à-vis* the rest of the globe over the last five hundred years, European literature has occupied a place of great prominence on the world stage. It has, unarguably, given rise to a great humanistic tradition. It has given us fantastic images of the world of struggle, of great upheavals, of change, of movement. When Shakespeare's King Lear breaks down under the storm occasioned by the fact of the old feudal order and conception of nature being challenged to the roots by the new bourgeois conception of nature and asks, who is that can tell me who I am, or the assasins in *Julius Ceasar*, bathing themselves in the blood of the victim, and one of them wondering how many times their deeds would be duplicated in the world in times and states as yet unborn, could they not have been painting images of the twentieth century? When Adam and Eve are taken by the angel Gabriel on to a hill just before their expulsion from paradise in Milton's *Paradise Lost* and are shown visions of the world to be; they are actually being given a global vision of all the cities and civilisations of the world among which are the great African empires of Songhay and the twelfth-century city states along the Kenyan coast of such as Malindi and Mombasa.

The humanistic side of European literature reflects of course the democratic social struggles of the European peoples. But given the domination of the West over the rest of the world through such repressive historical moments as the slave trade and slavery, colonialism and currently neo-colonialism, this literature tends to opt for silence or ambivalence or downright collaboration. Of course there are writers who show great sensitivity to the social evils perpetrated against other peoples: William Blake, Walt Whitman, Brecht, Sartre for instance. But taken as a whole this literature could not avoid being affected by the Eurocentric basis of its world view or global vision, and most of it, even when sympathetic, could not altogether escape from the racism inherent in Western enterprise in the rest of the world.

The nearer we come to the twentieth century, the more this literature seems ambivalent to the humanity of those struggling from outside the borders of the West. To illustrate my point, I shall choose four texts which fall quite easily into a canonised tradition of English literature. I am of course aware of the limitations of drawing a general conclusion from selected texts but the four texts are quite tempting because of the centrality of the figure of the colonised as perceived by the coloniser. Further, I merely want to illustrate a tendency and not make a literary evaluation.

The evolution and transformation of the figure of Caliban in English literature is a good example, in fact quite a revelation, of this tendency. We meet Caliban in Shakespeare's *Tempest* in the seventeenth century. I need not go into the details of the drama. Everybody knows all about Prospero taking over the island previously presided over by Caliban and his mother Sycorax. The exchange between Prospero and Caliban focuses over the issue of language. Prospero reminds the hostile Caliban that it was he who gave Caliban a language:

> When thou didst not, savage,
> Know thine own meaning, but wouldst gabble like
> A thing most brutish, I endowed thy purposes
> With words that made them known

Note the assumption that Caliban's language was mere gabble. Caliban, if you remember, answers not by reminding Prospero that he too had a language, but by showing him the uses to which he had put his knowledge of Prospero's tongue.

> You taught me language; and my profit on 't
> Is, I know how to curse. The red plague rid you
> For learning me your language.

The play is interesting in that it has all the images that are later to be reworked into a racist tradition particularly in popular European literature about the colonised peoples: the savage as a rapist, lazy, a lover of whisky, stupid, cannibalistic. But the main thing is that Shakespeare does give to Caliban the capacity or the voice to say 'no'. Caliban is invested with energy. And remember that at the time, Europe has occupied only a little corner of the globe.

We meet Caliban in a different guise in the early eighteenth century, say in the character of Friday in Daniel Defoe's *Robinson Crusoe*. Again the story of the shipwrecked Robinson Crusoe is well known. But note the process of Crusoe conferring humanity on

15

Friday. It is done through language. When they first meet, Friday does actually utter or speak some words and Crusoe, the narrator, is sufficiently moved to say that though 'I could not understand them, yet I thought they were pleasant to hear'. But in subsequent encounters between the teacher and the student, we never really get to hear more about Friday having a language:

> In a little time I began to speak to him and teach him to speak to me; and first I made him know that his name was Friday which was the day I saved his life . . . I likewise taught him to say Master, and then let him know that was to be my name.

And now see the results:

> I was greatly pleased with him and made it my business to teach him everything that was proper to make him useful, handy, and helpful; but especially to make him speak and understand me when I spake; and he was the aptest scholar that ever was, and particularly was so merry, so constantly diligent, and so pleased when he could but understand me or make me understand him, that it was very pleasant to talk to him.

Defoe has the usual images of cannibalism, tribal wars and savagery; but Friday also is given a voice; he is, for instance, made to doubt some of Crusoe's explanation of the origins of the universe. But there is no language of revolt, nothing closely resembling the energy of the seventeenth-century Caliban. And remember that by this time Europe has occupied a bit more of the globe and Africa has become a hunting ground for what resulted in one of the biggest forced mass exodus of peoples in history. Nor of course to forget the millions killed in the process.

We move to another text which covers the nineteenth century and the years of entry into the twentieth century. The text, *Heart of Darkness* by Joseph Conrad, was first published in 1902. By this time colonialism has become policy and the world is divided among a handful of oppressor nations. To be sure, Conrad's text is one of the most gripping evocations of the horror of imperialism particularly in its colonial guise. He debunks all the do-goodness associated with the nineteenth-century European colonial enterprise in Africa.

He is even aware of the racism inherent in such enterprises. Through the character of the narrator, there is this very telling comment:

> They were no colonists; their administration was merely a squeeze and nothing more, I suspect. They were conquerors, and for that you only want brute force – nothing to boast of, when you have it, since your strength is just an accident arising from the weakness of others. They grabbed what they could get for the sake of what was to be got. It was just robbery with violence, aggravated murder on a great scale, and men going at it blind. The conquest of the earth, which mostly means the taking it away from those who have a different complexion or slightly flatter noses than ourselves, is not a pretty thing when you look into it too much.

In the text there is no individual Caliban. Here Conrad assumes the collective figure of those Africans who accompany Marlowe into the interior of the continent. They are not given a voice, except, indirectly, through the narrator when they express a wish to eat their enemies. They have otherwise been divested of all energy. The only words uttered are by a Westernised boy, an Ariel figure, who announces: Mr Kurtz, he dead.

The fourth text was published in 1987 and it is by Coetzee, of European descent, born in South Africa, this last outpost of empire. He reworked the Friday story in the novel he called *Foe*, which was the original name of Daniel Defoe. One would have thought that Coetzee living in South Africa would bring new and exciting insights into the relationships between the coloniser and the colonised. The novel comes out after Sharpeville, after Soweto, and in the midst of the armed struggle waged by the African people under Umkhonto we Sizwe. But that is not the point. What interests me is that here Friday's tongue is actually pulled out. He has no tongue, no voice, no language, and hardly any energy. Coetzee's twentieth-century Friday, written on the eve of South African peoples' fierce determination to get rid of European domination, is a far cry from the energy of protest and self affirmation in Shakespeare's seventeenth-century Caliban created at a time when South Africa was only beginning to be the object of plunder by European powers.

The authors of the four texts could not be accused of being in sympathy with the European colonial enterprise. If anything, they are opposed or at the very least sceptical. But they carry in themselves a collaborationist tendency while they remain outside the central stream of conciously collaborationist letters.

The collaborationist literature, mostly popular literature, was downright racist. I shall not here dwell on this since it has been discredited enough in all serious discourse. Its very simplism speaks loudly enough about its intentions. The African was often depicted in the diametrically opposed polarities of the good and the bad, the noble and the savage. The good, the noble and the intelligent was the character who co-operated with the colonial process. The bad and the ugly was the African who opposed colonialism.

Thus, if people were really to depend on European literature, even at its best, they would get a very distorted picture of the modern world, its evolution and its contemporary being. The twentieth century is a product of imperialist adventurism, true, but also of resistance from the people of the Third World. This resistance is often reflected in the literature of the Third World and it is an integral part of the modern world, part of the forces which have been creating and are still creating the heritage of a common culture. They come from Asia. They come from South America. They come from Africa. And they come from the oppressed national sectors and social strata in North America, Australasia and Europe. The Third World is all over the world. There is of course no absolute uniformity in this literature and within itself as a modern tradition, a twentieth-century tradition, it carries all sorts of tendencies. Let me concentrate on literature from the African continent.

There are, as you know, three traditions in the literature from Africa. First is that of the oral tradition or orature. It is the literature passed on from mouth to ear, generation to generation. It consists of songs, poems, drama, proverbs, riddles, sayings and it is the richest and oldest of heritages. Furthermore, it is still very much alive and readily incorporates new elements. It can be extremely simple or very complex depending on the time, place and the occasion. I can think of no better demonstration of this tradition than in the remarkable recording of the *Ozidi Saga* by J.P Clark. Here the epic of Ozidi and his grandmother Oreame is told over a period of seven nights. The section dealing with the education of the epic hero, Ozidi, by his very demanding grandmother, is a remarkable example of narrative in orature while the scene involving the empowerment of Ozidi illustrates even more remarkably the fusion of theatre, drama, poetry, magic, ritual, music, song, audience participation, the real and the marvellous in orature. Among the Agĩkũyũ of Kenya there used to be a Gĩkũyũ poetry festival, or shall I say, competition, which drew large crowds. The best poets of the various regions would meet in the arena, like in a battle, and compete with words and instant compositions. These poets had even developed a form of hierographics which they kept to themselves. This kind of festival was killed by the British for they did not want crowds of people meeting and practising things that they, in the colonial administration, could not understand. The importance of the oral tradition is that through it's agency African languages in their most magical form have been kept alive. One of the highest developments of this was the *griot* tradition in West Africa. Whole epics and histories of families and nations were banked in the memories of these keepers of the word.

The second tradition is that of Africans writing in European languages particularly in those of the former colonisers. This is clearly a product of the fatal encounter between Africa and Europe in two ways. First is the question of language choice and this links it inevitably to the literatures carried by European languages. This literature is branded with the Europeanness of the word. A case of black skins in white linguistic masks? Secondly, it arose out of and was generally inspired by the great anti-colonial resistance of the African masses. Much of the literature was initially often a reaction to the conception of the universe in European literature in which the African was depicted as the negation of history. It had done a remarkable job in re-drawing the images of the world as previously drawn by the literature of Europe. It has rescued the world defined by European languages from the total grip of Eurocentrism. But in another sense it continued and even aided in that Eurocentrism by its very choice of languages. In other words it does not really matter how much Caliban is able to curse in European languages. He can do very remarkable things with it as we can see in *The Tempest*, in that great poetic evocation of Caliban's love of the island and his total identification with its landscape. But in so far as he has not been forced to abandon his language, as happened in the case of the African diaspora, he is accepting Prospero's racist assumptions about

19

the universe and contributing to Prospero's linguistic universe. He accepts that only by adopting the European tongue can he manage to express his humanity adequately. He has colluded in Prospero's uprooting of the African tongue à la Coetzee; the African peasant and worker in this literature reappears on the stage of world history speaking not his gabble but perfect English, French or Portuguese, a remarkable case of literary surgery and transplant since in reality the masses of African people do continue speaking and using and creating in African languages. Note that the new Caliban comes to Prospero's linguistic high table with an offering, a linguistic bottle of wine so to speak. Thus, this tradition has tried to forge an identity by borrowing very heavily from African languages, that is from the rich harvest of orature as developed by African languages over the years. But note also that Caliban is not borrowing from Prospero to enrich his own gabble. On the contrary. He sees his role as that of borrowing from his own gabble to enlarge the possibilities of Prospero's languages. He gives nothing, absolutely nothing, back to his languages. This ultimately is the tragedy of the Europhone tradition which has come to wear the mask of African literature. It is now a case of black skins in white masks wearing black masks.

In the area of economics and geography, it is the raw materials of gold, diamonds, coffee, tea, which are taken from Africa and processed in Europe and then resold to Africa. In the area of culture, the raw material of African orature and histories developed by African languages are taken, repackaged through English or French or Portuguese and then resold back to Africa. In both cases one is not questioning the quality of the products for this is not really what is at issue.

The third tradition is that of Africans writing in African languages. In the pre-colonial era, this was a minority tradition among the nations in that not many of the African languages had been reduced to writing. But it has always been there and as Professor Abiola Irele has pointed out it is these languages which contain the classical era of African literature, a pre-colonial tradition. It is the one that owns the label, the title, the name, 'African literature'. It has been overshadowed by the more recent Europhone tradition. But African languages are coming back. The language debate has dominated every single literature conference to do with Africa over the last few years and it is going to continue to do so with even greater aggressive insistence as we face the twenty-first century. To the old voices of Cheikh Anita Diop and David Diop calling for reconnection with that tradition are newer voices from the oral tradition adding to the continental chorus of concern. The Somali poet of the oral tradition, Mohamed Ismail of Garce, has gone so far as to accuse the educated Africans of committing treason against their own languages:

> Oh my friends, the Somali language is very perplexed;
> It is all anxiety in its present condition;
> The value of its words and expressions are being gagged by its own people;
> Its very back and hips are broken, and it accuses its own speakers of neglect;
> It is weeping with deep sorrow;
> It is being orphaned and its value is vanishing.

A reconnection with the classic tradition of our languages to express the contemporary world will not be an easy, 'walkover' kind of task. Writing in African languages has many difficulties and problems. Problems of literacy. Problems of publishing. Problems of the lack of a critical tradition. Problems of orthography. Problems of having very many languages in the same country. Problems of hostile governments with a colonised mentality. Abandonment by some of those who could have brought their genius – demonstrated by their excellent performance in foreign languages – to develop their own languages.

In short, literature in African languages suffers from a lack of a strong tradition, creative and critical. Writers in African languages are having to create several traditions simultaneously; publishing, critical vocabulary, orthography, and even words. But it has the advantage of being able to establish a natural give and take relationship to the rich heritage of orature. African writers in African languages are giving something back, however tiny, to the development of African languages.

That is why I still believe that despite the hue and cry about reductionism, nativism, backwardlookingness from the Europhonist opponents of this development, writing in African languages still holds the key for the positive development of new and vital traditions in African literature as we face the twenty-first century. Many

21

more people are facing up to the creative necessity of writing in African languages and to do for African languages what Spenser, Shakespeare and Milton did for English; what Cervantes did for Spanish; what Rabelais did for French; what Martin Luther, Goethe and Schiller did for the German language; what Pushkin, Gogol and Tolstoy did for Russian; what Elias Lonnrot of the Finnish classic, the *Kalevala*, did for Finnish; indeed what all writers in history have done for their languages. In short they are hearkening to the rescue call by the Somali poet quoted earlier.

African writers in African languages are engaged in the great adventure and drama of creating a new and great tradition. In this task they have at least two great reservoirs: the heritages of orature and of world literature and culture.

All great national literatures have rooted themselves in the culture and language of the peasantry. The Homeric *Iliad* and *Odessey*, as was all Greek drama, were rooted in the legends and stories that everybody knew. The Russian writers of the nineteenth century, particularly Pushkin, rooted their work in the culture of the peasantry. The *Kalevala*, the founding text of modern Finnish literature and language, was rooted in the folklore of the peasantry. The oral tradition will then be the basis or the foundation of the new tradition in African literature.

African languages must not be afraid of also borrowing from the best in world culture. All the dynamic cultures of the world have borrowed from other cultures in a process of mutual fertilisation. In his very interesting essay on the relationships between languages and cultures *From the Prehistory of Novelistic Discourse*, Bakhtin has this to say on the development of Latin:

> Latin literary language in all its generic diversity was created in the light of Greek literary language. Its national distinctiveness and the specific verbal thought process inherent in it were realised in creative literary consciousness in a way that would have been absolutely impossible under conditions of monoglossia. After all it is possible to objectivise one's own particular language, its internal form, the peculiarities of its world view, its special linguistic habitus only in the light of another language belonging to somebody else, which is almost as much 'one's own' as one's own native language.

22

One could add the rhetorical question: and is it possible to conceive of the development of Greek literature and culture without Egyptian and other Mediterranean cultures? African languages, as we have seen, have contributed immensely to the development of European languages and extended their possibilities through the Europhone literary tradition of the modern African experience. Indeed the new *Oxford English Dictionary* has canonised quite a number of new words from Kiswahili and other African languages.

African languages will borrow from one another; they will borrow from their classical heritages; they will borrow from the world – from the Caribbean, from Afroamerica, from Latin America, from the Asian – and from the European worlds. In this, the new writing in African languages will do the opposite of the Europhone practice: instead of being appropriated by the world, it will appropriate the world and one hopes on terms of equal exchange, at the very least, borrow on its own terms and needs.

The growth and the development of the new African literature in African languages will have vast implications for critical scholarship. Currently no expert on the so-called 'African literature' need ever show even the slightest acquaintance with any African language. Can you imagine a professor of French literature and culture who does not know a single word of French? Unfortunately it is not just the case of non-African scholars. African scholars of African realities need never show any acquaintance with African languages, even with their mother tongues. An African-languages-based critical scholarship would have a very vital role to play in the further development of the new African literature. The Europhone would occupy its proper place; as an appendage of European literature or as a footnote in African literature.

It is these revitalised African languages rooting themselves in the traditions of orature and of written African literature, inspired by the deepest aspirations of the African people for a meaningful social change, which will also be best placed to give and receive from the wealth of our common culture on an equal basis.

Similar cases can be made for the literature of Asia and South America over the last four hundred years. These literatures growing in the shadow of both great classical pasts and of European literatures, sometimes bitterly resisting their appeal, at other times borrowing from them, but absorbing the borrowed features to create their unique traditions, creating so to speak their own space in a world dominated by cultural imperialism from the West, all add to the literature and culture of resistance. They are an integral part of what makes up the twentieth century and the foundation of the literature and cultures of the twenty-first century. The languages and literatures of Asia, Africa and South America, the literatures of peoples of non-European stock but who are now part of the economic, political and cultural reality of the West, are all creating space for a hundred flowers to bloom on a global scale; and the organisation of cultural studies all over the world should reflect this multi-coloured reality of the human creative stream. The continued domination of the world by a handful of European languages and literatures can only make the world poorer not richer. The transition in African, Asian, South American, North American and European letters is towards traditions that will freely give and take, on the basis of equality and mutual respect, from this vast heritage of human creativity.

The wealth of a common global culture will then be expressed in the particularities of our different languages and cultures very much like a universal garden of many-coloured flowers. The 'flowerness' of the different flowers is expressed in their very diversity. But there is cross-fertilisation between them. And what is more they all contain in themselves the seeds of a new tomorrow.

3 The Universality of Local Knowledge

There are two reasons why I am drawn towards Professor Geertz's emphasis on the importance of local knowledge or of starting from the particular to the general. As a writer, a novelist, I like to see, in the words of William Blake, 'the world in a grain of sand', or in those of an African proverb quoted by Professor Geertz in his book *Local Knowledge: Fact and Law in Comparative Perspective*, 'to get wisdom from an ant heap'. A novelist is almost wholly dependent on the particular. Whatever he may have to say about life, it must be rooted in the particularities of daily experience. Coming from that part of the globe, called, for lack of a better word, the Third World, I am suspicious of the uses of the word and the concept of the universal. For very often, this has meant the West generalising its experience of history as the universal experience of the world. What is Western becomes universal and what is Third World becomes local. Locality becomes measured by the degree of its distance from the metropolis of the Western world. Thus Professor Geertz's warning about the relativity of terms, even of the local and the universal, is timely, for, in our case, the Eurocentric basis of seeing the world has often meant marginalising into the periphery that which comes from the rest of the world. One historical particularity is generalised into a timeless and spaceless universality. In that sense, shifting the focus of particularity to a plurality of centres, is a welcome antidote.

However, I share Professor Goody's unease about the tendency to see the universal and the local in absolute opposition to each other. Professor Geertz talks of confusion in the social and human sciences over three notions, of the universal, the generalisation, and the law. Again he talks as if the three categories are mutually opposed, which

25

in fact goes against the logic of his observation about wisdom coming from an ant heap. The ant heap is particular. Wisdom is a generalisation tending towards the universal codified into a proverb. The process of cognition begins with noting, observing the particular and then working out what is general from the particular. From the general, a regulating principle, a law, emerges which can take the form of the universal. The universal, the law, and the general are then tested against the ground of particularity in practice. Practice is both the starting point and the testing ground of our conceptualisation of the world. What is needed is not so much the recovery of practical philosophy as the recovery of the philosophy of practice.

The problem arises from the tendency to see the local and the universal in mechanical opposition; and the relativity of cultures in a temporal ground of equality almost as if cultures within a nation and between nations have developed on parallel bars towards parallel ends that never meet, or if they meet, they do so in infinity. The universal is contained in the particular just as the particular is contained in the universal. We are all human beings but the fact of our being human does not manifest itself in its abstraction but in the particularity of real living human beings of different climes and races. We can talk of the human capacity for languages but that capacity manifests itself in real concrete languages as spoken by different peoples of the earth. In other words, we realise language as a universal human phenomenon not in its abstract universality but in its particularity as the different languages of the earth. Even the limited universality of a single language, say English, is realised through the language as actually spoken. But it is also from the particularity of these numerous utterances that we can recognise general features that can make us talk of English as a language different from, say, Kiswahili. There are other categories in Professor Geertz's statement and from other pieces that reinforce this tentative feeling that he tends to emphasise mutual opposition of phenomena instead of seeing the linkages and therefore the real differences. I agree with Professor Goody that meaning and machinery are not necessarily opposed absolutes. The hydrologist may very well be a swimmer. At any rate if there is no water there can never be a swimmer and the hydrologist who can make possible the realisation of actual water may be the maker of a swimmer.

Which brings me to my last observation. Culture develops within the process of a people wrestling with their natural and social environment. They struggle with nature. They struggle with one another. They evolve a way of life embodied in their institutions and certain practices. Culture becomes the carrier of their moral, aesthetic and ethical values. At the psychological level, these values become the embodiment of the people's consciousness as a specific community. That consciousness in turn has an effect on how they look at their values, at their culture, at the organisation of power, and at the organisation of their wealth extracted from nature through the mediation of their labour. Within a given community any change in any of the major aspects of their lives, how they manage their wealth for instance, or their power, may well bring about changes at all the other levels and these in turn will bring about mutual action and reaction on all the other aspects. Here there is no stillness but constant movement and the problem with the study of cultures, no matter from what academic centre, is how to study them in their movement and linkages to other processes in that society or community. It is like studying a river in its very movement, that is in its very being as a river. What I noted, or thought I noted, in Professor Geertz's statement is the almost total exclusion of notions of struggle, movement and change.

But cultures do not always develop out of the workings-out of contradictions within themselves or with the other features of that society only. They also develop in an external environment of contact with other societies. This contact can be one of hostility, indifference, or of mutual give and take. The same is of course true of the development in thought and even in academic disciplines. There are internal arguments within a discipline and also arguments arising from contact with other thoughts and disciplines bringing about sometimes what Professor Geertz has elsewhere argued as the blurring of genres or the refiguration of social thought.

Over the last four hundred years the developments in the West have not just been the result of internal social dynamics, but also their relationship with Africa, Asia and South America. But both the internal relationships within them and their external relations with Africa, Asia and South America, have not been those of equality but of dominance and domination at the economic, political and cultural levels. The slave trade and slavery bringing about mass relocation of peoples; colonialism bringing about immense economic, political, cultural and psychological violence on colonised communities, have meant that there is no culture which has not been affected adversely or otherwise by those relationships of dominance and domination. But they have also been affected by the traditions of resistance from the dominated. This external domination and the resistance to it can be parallelled, in the colonised communities and in the dominating nations, with the internal disempowerment of peoples and resistance to this. Any study of cultures which ignores structures of domination and control and resistance within nations and between nations and races over the last four hundred years is in danger of giving a distorted picture. Western scholarship for instance has not escaped from the racism which necessarily arose out of those structures. Disciplines like anthropology and ethnography initially meant the study of those remote communities which seem to have some remote resemblance to 'ours'; perhaps they are the missing social link to 'our' arrival at the twentieth century of 'the West and the rest of us', to borrow a phrase from Chinweizu's book of the same title. The persistence of a certain vocabulary – the primitive, the tribal community, simpler societies is a reminder of the remote kinship between scholarship and colonialism. Even the organisation of disciplines and syllabi can be affected by that history. Over the last so many years voices from those nations and sectors of the communities which were dominated have been speaking out, naming their world so to speak. But what has been the place of African literatures, African languages, African political and philosophic thought in the organisation of departments that house various disciplines? The world of academic study is still almost wholly dominated by that which has been initiated from the languages and centres of power in the West.

This does not mean that societies cannot be studied by people from other communities. But whether studying other communities, our communities or any other social phenomenon, it is important to see phenomenon in nature, society, even in academia, not in its isolation but in its dynamic connections with other phenomena. It is important to remember that social and intellectual processes, even academic disciplines, act and react on each other not against a spatial and temporal ground of stillness but of constant struggle, of movement, and change which brings about more struggle, more movement, and change, even in human thought.

In a situation of flux, the effective use of the delicate skills of navigating our way through may very well depend on whether we are swimming against or with the currents of change or for that matter whether we are clear in what direction we are swimming, towards or away from the sea of our connections with our common humanity. Local knowledge is not an island unto itself; it is part of the main, part of the sea. Its limits lie in the boundless universality of our creative potentiality as human beings.

4 *Imperialism of Language*

English, a Language for the World?

Everyone in the world has a language, either the language of his or her parents or one adopted at birth or at a later stage in life. So when we consider English as a possible language for the world, we are all drawing from the languages and cultures in which we are rooted. The topic also brings up the question of choosing one language from among many languages. What we are therefore discussing is the relationship between English and the various languages of the world. In short, we are really talking about the meeting of languages.

Every language has two aspects. One aspect is its role as an agent that enables us to communicate with one another in our struggle to find the means for survival. The other is its role as a carrier of the history and the culture built into the process of that communication over time. In my book *Decolonising the Mind* I have described language as the collective memory bank of a people. The two aspects are inseparable; they form a dialectical unity.

However, either of these two aspects can become more pronounced than the other, depending in the circumstances surrounding the use of a language, and particularly those surrounding an encounter between languages. For instance, are the two languages meeting on terms of equality and independence? The quality of the encounter between languages both in the past and in the world today, and hence the dominance of one aspect over the other at a given time, has been determined by the presence or absence of independence and quality between the nations involved.

Let me give one or two examples. Scandinavians know English. But they do not learn English in order for it to become the means of communication among themselves in their own countries, or for it to become the carrier of their own national cultures, or for it to become the means by which foreign culture is imposed on them. They learn English to help them in their interactions with English people, or with speakers of English, to facilitate commerce, trade, tourism, and other links with foreign nations. For them English is only a means of communication with the outside world. The Japanese, the West Germans, and a good number of other peoples fall in the same category as the Scandinavians: English is not a substitute for their own languages.

When nations meet on terms of independence and equality, they tend to stress the need for communication in the language of the other. They choose the language of the other merely to ease communication in their dealings with one another. But when they meet as oppressor and oppressed, as for instance under imperialism, then their languages cannot experience a genuinely democratic encounter. The oppressor nation uses language as a means of entrenching itself in the oppressed nation. The weapon of language is added to that of the Bible and the sword in pursuit of what David Livingstone, in the case of nineteenth-century imperialism, called 'Christianity plus 5 percent.' Today he would have probably described the same process as Christianity, debt, plus 40 percent in debt servicing. In such a situation, what is at stake is language as more than a simple means of communication.

Needless to say, the encounter between English and most so-called Third World languages did not occur under conditions of independence and equality. English, French, and Portuguese came to the Third World to announce the arrival of the Bible and the sword. They came clamouring for gold, black gold in chains, or gold that shines as sweat in factories and plantations. If it was the gun which made possible the mining of this gold and which effected the political captivity of their owners, it was language which held captive their cultures, their values, and hence their minds. The latter was attempted in two ways, both of which are part of the same process.

The first was to suppress the languages of the captive nations. The culture and the history carried by these languages were thereby thrown onto the rubbish heap and left there to perish. These languages were experienced as incomprehensible noise from the dark

Tower of Babel. In the secondary school that I went to in Kenya, one of the hymns we were taught to sing was a desperate cry for deliverance from that darkness. Every morning, after we paraded our physical cleanliness for inspection in front of the Union Jack, the whole school would troop down to the chapel to sing: 'Lead kindly light amidst the encircling gloom, lead thou me on.' Our languages were part of that gloom. Our languages were suppressed so that we, the captives, would not have our own mirrors in which to observe ourselves and our enemies.

The second mode of captivation was that of elevating the language of the conquerer. It became the language of the elect. Those inducted into the school system, after having been sifted from the masses of the people, were furnished with new mirrors in which to see themselves and their people as well as those who had provided the new mirrors. In short, they were given a language called English or French or Portuguese. Thus equipped with the linguistic means of escape from the dark Tower of Babel, the newly ordained, or those ready to be ordained as servants of the new order, had their minds systematically removed from the world and the history carried by their original languages. They looked, or were made to look, to a distant neon light on a faraway hill flashing out the word EUROPE. Henceforth Europe and its languages would be the centre of the universe.

The French, faithful to the philosophical and aesthetic traditions of their culture, had given the whole process a name: *assimilation*. The English, less aesthetically and philosophically inclined, simply called it *education*. But Lugard, a soldier-turned-administrator who nonetheless retained the bluntness of a military man, had provided the key to understanding what lay behind this pragmatic education programme, one that was often formulated in bits and pieces: *indirect rule*. He had coined the phrase to refer to the practice of co-opting chiefs to facilitate British rule in Africa. In fact, subsequent educational practice produced more faithful 'chiefs' for the system as a whole than those who had been appointed earlier by Lugard. The point however is that the mastery of the English language was the measure of one's readiness for election into the band of the elect.

In *Decolonising the Mind* I have described how the process of alienation from our own languages with the acquisition of a new one actually worked. I have told of instances of children being punished if they were caught speaking their African languages. We were often caned or made to carry plaques inscribed with the words 'I am stupid' or 'I am an ass'. In some cases, our mouths were stuffed with pieces of paper picked from the wastepaper basket, which were then passed from one mouth to that of the latest offender. Humiliation in relation to our languages was the key. 'Look up unto the hills' was the constant call: that was where the light from Europe shone, and the gateway to it was English. The English language was the bearer of all knowledge in the arts and sciences. According to Greek tradition, Archimedes could have moved the world had he had a firm ground on which to stand. In twentieth-century Africa he would have been advised to stand on the firm ground of the English language in order to move the world. Indeed for some of us, English was made to look as if it was the language spoken by God.

One of our English teachers, ironically a Scotsman, used to urge us to follow the footsteps of Christ in the use of the English language. As you know, when young people learn a new language, they tend to favour the heaviest and longest of words because such words sound more learned. The teacher would tell us that Jesus Christ used the simplest English. The Bible contained the greatest sentence in English literature which happened also to be the shortest. It was left to a student to remind him that Jesus probably spoke Hebrew, and that the Bible from which the King James Version had been translated, was more likely to have been written in Hebrew.*

You may think that I am talking about some attitudes to the English language that prevailed thirty years ago. Well, you are very wrong. Recently, on my way to Berlin with my mind very much on this seminar, I chanced to open the London *Evening Standard* of 7 October 1988, and came across an article concerning the British education secretary Kenneth Baker's visit to the Soviet Union. The paper told us how Baker had been amazed to find English being spoken in a certain part of the Soviet Union: 'Just think of it. There I was in Novosibirsk. Two thousand miles from anywhere, and yet the people could speak English perfectly. They've never been to England or America. But they read our classics.' That is well and

---

*I note that Christ spoke Aramaic and not Hebrew and that the New Testament was written in Greek. To correct the child's misconception is hardly to weaken his point, which retains its polemical truth with respect to the teacher's assumptions.

good. Any group learning the language of another group is a positive thing. But why were these citizens of Novosibirsk putting so much work into perfecting their English? According to Kenneth Baker, as quoted by the same issue of the *Standard*, there was a deeper motive: 'The Russians associate England with progress, so they work thoroughly and very hard at their English. They want to get away from the old-fashioned totalitarian state-controlled society.' You have heard it for yourselves. Socialism, which is only seventy years old, is already old-fashioned. Capitalism, which is four hundred years old, is modern. But the point to note for our argument is that even today English is the means of taking people away from the 'gloom' of socialism into the 'light' of modern capitalism.

Let me now relate to you very briefly how some of us were taken by English from the dark Babelic towers of nineteenth-century Africa to the modernity of twentieth-century colonial Africa. In my primary school we were taught English from a text under the general series 'Oxford Readers for Africa'. We used to read the story of a boy called John and a girl called Joan. And it thus came to pass that, while still in my village and before I knew the names of any other towns in Kenya, I already knew about a town called Oxford where the two children were born and another called Reading, where John and Joan went to school. We, the new readers, followed them wherever they went. One day we went to visit another town called London; we went to a zoo and walked along the banks of the river Thames. It was a summer holiday. Oh, how many times did the river Thames and the British Houses of Parliament beckon to us from the pages of our English language text books! Even today, when I hear the name of the river Thames or travel in its vicinity, I still remember Joan and John. And Oxford represents to me less the great seat of exclusive scholarship that it is supposed to be than the exclusive home of the fictitious John and Joan of my primary school textbook.

Don't get me wrong. I do not think it a bad thing for a language to be taught in the geographical, cultural, or historical setting of the land which produces it. After all, even the communicative aspect of a language cannot be divorced from its cultural emblems – the Thames for the English language, the Eiffel Tower for the French, the Leaning Tower of Pisa for the Italian, the Great Wall of China for the Chinese, Mecca for the Arabic, Mombasa for the Kiswahili. To know a language in the context of its culture is a tribute to the people to whom it belongs, and that is good. What has, for us from the former colonies, twisted the natural relation to languages, both our own and those of other peoples, is that the languages of Europe – here, English – were taught as if they were our own languages, as if Africa had no tongues except those brought there by imperialism, bearing the label MADE IN EUROPE.

Thus English and the African languages never met as equals, under conditions of equality, independence, and democracy, and this is the root of all subsequent distortions. They met with English as the language of the conquering nation, and ours as the language of the vanquished. An oppressor language inevitably carries racist and negative images of the conquered nation, particularly in its literature, and English is no exception. I do not want to go into this aspect of the language here. Many studies in this area have already been done. Suffice it to say that some works bearing these offensive images, like those of Elspeth Huxley, Karen Blixen, Rider Haggard, Robert Ruark, Nicholas Monsarrat, to name just a few, found their way into the school English curriculum. Imagine it: if the African languages had all died, African people would have had to define themselves in a language that had such a negative conception of Africa as its legacy.

What prevented our languages from being completely swallowed up by English and other oppressor languages was that the rural and urban masses, who had refused to surrender completely in the political and economic spheres, also continued to breathe life into our languages and thus helped to keep alive the histories and cultures they carried. The masses of Africa would often derive the strength needed in their economic and political struggles from those very languages. Thus the peoples of the Third World had refused to surrender their souls to English, French, or Portuguese.

But the Third World was not the only place where English tried to grow on the graveyard of other peoples' languages. Even in Britain I have heard similar complaints from regions whose original languages had been swallowed up by English or in regions where they are putting up a last ditch struggle to prevent their languages from being killed and buried forever.

Once again, I am not only talking about complaints that I heard

35

many years ago. When I returned from West Berlin, I happened to open a newspaper, the *Morning Star* of 21 October 1988, only to find an article by Lyn Marierid of the Welsh Language Society protesting the continuing decline of the Welsh language:

> In recent years, rural areas, which have for decades been considered strongholds of the language, have become completely Anglicised as ordinary working-class people have been systematically priced out of their native areas.
>
> Perhaps some readers are asking at this point why it should be so important to retain such a language as Welsh.
>
> If we consider it important for a people to be aware of their past in order to be able to shape their future, then it is pointedly relevant. For generations, the Welsh working class was utterly dependent on the Welsh language and culture.
>
> Now it appears that the Welsh language in Wales is under threat of death. That, indeed, is the cost of 'yuppiefication' in this particular part of Britain. Should it die, then the history of a whole people would be a closed book for many people.
>
> As socialists we know that capitalist culture seeks to deny working people their rightful place in their own history so that it may not be a source of inspiration for their continued struggle in the present.
>
> Language too is denied them for similar reasons.
>
> Languages do not grow, age and die. They do not become irrelevant to the 'modern age' due to some intrinsic fault in their composition.
>
> They are lost when the predominant class in society has no use for them.

The decline of the Welsh language has roots in the inequality prevailing between the nationalities that inhabited the two linguistic regions. Even Kenneth Baker, when talking about the spread of English in Russia, did not say, from what one gathers in reading the report in the *Evening Standard*, that the Soviets looked up to Britain for progress. They looked to England, the original home of the English language.

Today, the West European languages and African languages are where they are in relation to one another, not because they are inherently progressive or backward but because of the history of oppression on one hand, and the resistance to that oppression on the other. That history of oppression dates back a long time, but it is best symbolised by the Berlin Conference of 1884 at which Africa, for example, was carved up into various 'spheres of influence' of the European powers. Today we can see that English, outside its home base in Britain and the United States, has firmly taken root in all respects only in those areas of the globe – and these are quite considerable – which have been within the Anglo-American economic and political empire stretching from Queen Victoria to Ronald Reagan. These are also the areas in which neo-colonialism has taken firm root. The rulers of these neo-colonies feel that they share the same outlook as the rulers of the United States and Britain because, quite apart from many other things they have in common, they speak the same tongue and share the value systems of the English-speaking ruling classes the world over.

The consequences of that history of inequality and oppression can be seen in each of the affected countries in Africa, particularly in the internal relations between the various classes and in the external relations with other countries. In these countries, English, French, and Portuguese occupy the centre stage. They are the official languages of instruction, of administration, of commerce, trade, justice, and foreign communications. In short, they are the languages of power. But they are still spoken only by a minority within each of the nationalities that make up these countries. The majority of the working people in Africa retain our African languages. Therefore the majority of the people are excluded from centre stage since they do not have mastery of the language of power. They are also excluded from any meaningful participation in modern discoveries. English, French, and Portuguese are the languages in which the African people have been educated; for this reason the results of our research into science, technology and of our achievements in the creative arts are stored in those languages. Thus a large portion of this vast knowledge is locked up in the linguistic prison of English, French, and Portuguese. Even the libraries are really English (or indeed French or Portuguese) language fortresses inaccessible to the majority. So the cultivation of these languages makes for more effective communication only between the elite and the international English-speaking bourgeoisie. In short the elite in Africa is, in linguistic terms, completely uprooted from the peoples of Africa and tied to the West.

As for external relations between Africa and the world, African languages hardly occupy any place of honour. Once again their place has been occupied by English, French, or Portuguese. Among the official languages at the United Nations there is not a single language of African origin. In fact it is interesting that of the five continents, the only one not represented linguistically at the United Nations is Africa. It is surely time that Kiswahili, or Hausa, Wolof, Shona, Amharic, or Somali be made one of the official languages of the United Nations Organisation and all its. organs; but that is a matter for another seminar. At present we are discussing English as a possible language for the world.

I have so far discussed or pointed out only the racist tradition of the English language. As a language of imperialism, it could not but be marked by the very disease it carried. But as the language of the people of Britain and America, it also has a democratic tradition, reflecting the democratic struggles and heritage of the British and American people. In its democratic tradition it has added to the common pool of human creativity; in the arts, for instance, with such great names as Shakespeare, Milton, Blake, Shelley, Dickens, Conrad, Bernard Shaw, Graham Greene, to name only a few. I am not surprised that Kenneth Baker found Soviet children in Siberia reading some of these classics of the English language. If he had also gone to even the remotest village in Africa he might very well have found more children struggling with Dickens, alongside Brecht, Balzac, Sholokhov, and of course Sembene Ousmane, Alex la Guma, Veiera, and other African writers. A lot of this material would be available in English translation. That side of the English language is important, and it is part of the common heritage of humankind along with what has been contributed by other languages, including those from Africa. But English as a language for the world is another matter.

English, a language for the world? It would certainly be good for each country in the world to have a language in which all nationalities inhabiting its boundaries could participate. It would be equally good if the world had a language in which all the nations of the earth could communicate. A common language of communication within a country, a common language of communication for the world: that is the ideal, and we have to struggle for it.

But that language, whichever it would be, should not be planted in the graveyard of other languages within one country or in the world. We must avoid the destruction that English has wrought on other languages and cultures in its march to the position it now occupies in the world. The death of many languages should never be the condition for the life of a few. On the contrary, the lives of many languages should add life to whichever language emerges as the transnational or universal language of communication between people. We, the present generation, must distance ourselves from the false and bloody logic of development theory handed to us by imperialism: the claim that the cleanliness of one person must depend on pouring dirt onto others; that the health of a few must depend on their passing their leprosy onto others; that the wealth of a few people or a few nations must be rooted in the poverty of the masses of people and nations.

So, what would be the proper foundation for the emergence and the universal acceptance of a language for the world?

First, the absolute independence and equality of all nations in the economic, political, and cultural spheres. Such an equality would of course be reflected in the equality of languages. We live in one world. All the languages in the world are real products of human history.

They are our common heritage. A world of many languages should be like a field of flowers of different colours. There is no flower which becomes more of a flower on account of its colour or its shape. All such flowers express their common 'floralness' in their diverse colours and shapes. In the same way our different languages can, should, and must express our common being. So we should let all our languages sing of the unity of the people of the earth, of our common humanity, and above all of the people's love for peace, equality, independence, and social justice. All our languages should join in the demand for a new international economic, political, and cultural order.

Then the different languages should be encouraged to talk to one another through the medium of interpretation and translation. Each country should encourage the teaching of languages from the five continents of the earth. There is no reason why each child should not master at least three languages as a matter of course. The art of translation and interpretation should be an integral subject in schools, but it is sad to note that in the English education system and in English culture generally, the art of translation does not enjoy the same status as the other arts. Through translations, the different languages of the world can speak to one another. European languages have always communicated with one another such that today it is possible to read nearly all the classics of Russian, French, or German literature and philosophy in any of those languages, thanks to the art of translation. But there is very little mutual translation between African languages and, say, English and French. And the colonial dominance of English and French in African lives has made African languages so suspicious of one another that there is hardly any inter-African communication. In any case, very few resources, if any, nationally or internationally, have been put into the development of African languages. The best minds among lettered Africans have been channelled into the developing of English, French, and Portuguese. But, difficult as the case may be, interlanguage communication through translation is crucial. If on top of all of this there were one common language, then the different languages of the world could further communicate with one another via the international common language. In that way, we could build a real foundation for a common world culture that is firmly rooted in, and draws its real sustenance from, all the peoples of the world with their distinct experiences and languages. Our internationalism would be truly rooted in all the peoples of the world.

When there is real economic, political, and cultural equality among nations and there is *democracy*, there will be no reason for any nation, nationality, or people to fear the emergence of a common language, be it Kiswahili, Chinese, Maori, Spanish, or English, as the language of the world. A language for the world? A world of languages! The two concepts are not mutually exclusive provided there is independence, equality, democracy, and peace among nations.

In such a world, English, like all the other languages, can put in an application, and despite its history of imperialist aggression against other languages and peoples, English would make a credible candidate. Such applicants must in the meantime work hard to remove such negative qualities as racism, sexism, national chauvinism, and negative images of other nationalities and races so as to meet the criteria of acceptance as a language for the world. In this respect Kiswahili would make an excellent candidate for the world language. It already has the advantage of never having grown in the graveyard of other languages. Kiswahili has created space for itself in Africa and the world without displaying any national chauvinism. The power of Kiswahili has not depended on its economic, political, or cultural aggrandisement. It has no history of oppression or domination of other cultures. And yet Kiswahili is now spoken as a major language in Eastern, Central, and Southern Africa as well as in many other parts of the world.

I have nothing against English, French, Portuguese, or any other language for that matter. They are all valid in as far as they are languages and in as far as they do not seek to oppress other nations, nationalities, and languages. But if Kiswahili or any other African language were to become the language for the world, this would symbolise the dawn of a new era in human relations between the nations and peoples of Africa and those of other continents. For these reasons I for one would like to propose Kiswahili as the language for the world.

Translated from the Gĩkũyũ by Wangũi wa Goro and Ngũgĩ wa Thiong'o.

5 *Cultural Dialogue for a New World*

Culture is a product of a peoples' history. But it also reflects that history and embodies a whole set of values by which a people view themselves and their place in time and space. Cultural contact can therefore play a great part in bringing about mutual understanding between peoples of different nations. Instead of armaments and nuclear weapons, instead of imposing one's own version of democracy on tiny islands and continents through Rapid or Low Deployment Forces, let people of the world dialogue together through culture.

But what culture are we talking about? Cultural contact on what basis? It is easy to identify two warring traditions of culture in Africa today.

First, the imperialist tradition. Imperialism, the conquest and the subjugation of the entire labour power of other countries by the concentrated capital, or moneypower, of another country came to realise that the economic exploitation and the political domination of a people could never be complete without cultural and hence mental and spiritual subjugation. The economic and political conquest of Africa was accompanied by cultural subjugation and the imposition of an imperialist cultural tradition whose dire effects are still being felt today.

Under colonialism this took the form of destroying peoples' languages, history, dances, education, religions, naming systems, and other social institutions that were the basis of their self-conception as a people. White adventurers and fortune hunters also stole precious works of art. Some of these stolen items can still be seen in many highly reputable museums in many capitals of the West. But more important in its negative consequences was the wholesale destruction of artistic creations; either melting them into bars of gold, or, fired by a crusading Christian zeal, simply burning them as symbols of witchcraft or graven images of the devil. Colonialism went for the flattening or fossilisation of its victims' cultures.

On this wasteland of its creation, colonialism erected an art in which Europe was always at the centre. In many paintings of the colonial period, the white adventurer was always at the centre of action with the rays of light radiating outwards from him. Africans were background shadows merging with the outer darkness and the natural landscape. A variation of the white theme in the arts was the presentation of a white God, Jesus, Virgin Mary and the angels in heaven as the universal religion. In schools, African students were encouraged to paint collaborators with colonialism in good positive colours. Where the figure of a possible black Jesus appeared, it was in his humble subservience to violence. Other dominant figures in such schools and colleges were of black Christian martyrs, a martyrdom conferred on the basis of their holy zeal in collaborating with the colonial enemies of their people. You will find a variation of the same theme in literature encouraged for use in the schools of the period. *Up From Slavery* by Booker T. Washington, a book that argued that slavery had actually been quite beneficial to black people was in many school libraries and classrooms all over Africa.

Finally this colonialism recognised as truly African only art and artistic activities which were completely emptied of all meaningful content. Thus lifeless carved figures of giraffes and elephants were paraded as authentically African just as empty acrobatic dancing and bodily contortions were similarly paraded for the colonial governor and visiting dignitaries. Thus colonialism was not entirely averse to associating itself to reactionary backward elements in peoples' cultures which it more often than not fossilised in museums or paraded as irrelevant, static traditionalism labelled as the authentic remnants and manifestation of true African culture.

The imperialist cultural tradition in its colonial form was meant to undermine peoples' belief in themselves and make them look up to the European cultures, languages and the arts, for a measurement of themselves and their abilities. It was meant to undermine their belief in their capacity to struggle successfully for control of their whole social and natural environment.

Unfortunately the same continues in the Africa of today. Independence which at the very least should have meant the liberation of a peoples' productive forces from foreign control was in most cases merely a change of form from colonial economic and political arrangement and practices to a more vicious neo-colonial arrangement. Some of these regimes have gone so far up the neo-colonial path that they have ceded their territory for use by US military forces; and thus for a small commission fee these regimes have put their entire populations at the mercy of whoever is occupying the White House. This is reflected in the new regimes' attitude to culture. What is, therefore, often officially paraded as authentic African culture today is virtually a repeat of the colonial tradition: tourist art, dances, acrobatic contortions emptied of the content of struggle, or else subservient theatre, music and film that always praises the leader as faultless and imbued with a wisdom that comes to him directly from heaven. This officially sanctioned African culture looks outwards for alliances in the most backward elements in Western culture.

But fortunately there is another tradition in African culture. This is a patriotic national tradition developing in resistance and opposition to imperialist-sanctioned African culture. Under colonialism this was a culture which through songs, dances, poetry, drama, spoke of and reflected peoples' real needs as they struggled against appalling working conditions in the settler-occupied farms and in factories or which sang of their hopes as they took up arms against colonial exploitation and political oppression. Whether in sculpture, poetry, songs, or dances, the patriotic arts looked to the past for progressive elements in form but always injected them with a new content born of the urgent present that raised them to a higher level. At the same time, the patriotic resistance arts were not afraid of incorporating new forms.

During the colonial period the practitioners of this culture were often jailed, maimed or even killed. Their songs, dances and even their sculptures were often banned. Colonial Kenya for instance saw such popular, but politically-conscious, dances and songs like Kanyegenyūri and Mūthīrīgū actually banned by the colonial authorities. Mau Mau writers and poets were jailed without trial or else killed. Unfortunately, even after independence the new regimes maintained this hostility to national patriotic cultures that reflected peoples' total opposition to the continued plunder of their labour and wealth by imperialism and its local black allies. Artists and writers belonging to this tradition have been jailed, maimed and killed. Peasant and worker-based theatre movements have been banned. Cultural centres built by the efforts of peasants and workers have been destroyed.

I am not talking of abstractions. Not so long ago, three truckloads of armed policemen were sent by the Moi–Kanu regime to Kamĩrĩĩthũ Community and Cultural Centre in Limuru, Kenya and razed the peoples' open-air theatre to the ground. The administration banned any theatre activities in the area. Yet the same regime was quite happy to sponsor Elspeth Huxley's televison version of her settler memoirs *Flame Trees of Thika* at about the same time that it was banning the Kenya peoples' interpretion of the same history. Thus a few months after my own play *Maitũ Njugĩra* was stopped, a worse fate met the author of the play, *Kilio cha haki*. Al Amin Mazrui was detained without trial for over two years at various maximum security prisons in the country after his play talking about the conditons of workers was performed at the University of Nairobi . . . Leading Kenyan writers like Abdulatif Abdulla, Kĩmani Gecau, Ngũgĩ wa Mĩriĩ, now live in exile. Yet the same regime will go cap in hand to Western capitals to seek aid, even for culture. So we cannot be talking about the same culture, even African culture, or are we?

Imperialism in its colonial form was not able to destroy a people's fighting culture. I can firmly say this: that Imperialism in its neo-colonial clothes will not be able to destroy the fighting culture of the African peasantry and working class for the simple reason that this culture is a product and a reflection of real life struggles going on in Africa today. You can destroy a people's culture completely only by destroying the people themselves and I suppose that we can safely leave that task to those who think that they can win a limited nuclear war so that they can continue to eat up, unmolested, uncontested, the resources of the people of Asia, Africa and South America.

The resistance culture and values of the African peasantry and working class have no basic contradiction with the democratic and humanistic cultures and values of the European and American peoples. These can hold a meaningful, fruitful dialogue. This is the dialogue and contact we must continue to aid, encourage and support by every means at our disposal. .

6 The Cultural Factor in the Neo-colonial Era

The two most obvious features of imperialism today are its neo-colonial form and the leadership of the USA. But the two are not entirely new in the history of modern imperialism.

The USA, or more precisely its constituent parts, was born in the era of the primitive accumulation of capital with the African based slave trade, slavery and semi-slavery being central. The USA's own capitalism begins its youthful stage with the declaration of independence and does not come of age until its political hegemony over the slave-owning rural economies of the southern States. This coincided with the high noon of laissez-faire capitalism in Europe, the era of industrial capitalism, with Britain boasting of its role as the workshop of the world.

The very triumph of the European laissez-faire capitalism with its increasing need for the security of the sources of raw materials and for control of both the home and foreign markets was already turning competition into its opposite: monopoly! European capitalism was entering its imperialist stage with monopoly at home and abroad becoming the national clarion call. The subsequent greed for colonies in Africa was barely covered by the verbal grandiloquence about discovery, exploration, missionary-do-goodness, telescopic philanthropy: it was simple national jingoism but quite profitable wearing the banner of spreading civilisation to the world. The symbol of the new turn in the fortunes of European capitalism was the 1884 Berlin conference which carved Africa up into colonies and spheres of influence of the various European powers and their capitalist associations. The USA's capitalism, emerging from its youthful stage to claims of adulthood was a keen observer at the conference.

Thus by the time the USA's capitalism matured into the imperialist stage, the world had already been divided into colonies and semicolonies of the rival European imperialisms. The USA could only turn to the newly independent countries of Central and South America which had been disengaging themselves from the weaker European powers of Portugal and Spain. Thus the passage of US capitalism into imperialism almost immediately took on a neo-colonial form. Between 1899 and 1917, the armed forces of the USA had intervened in at least seven South American countries and Caribbean islands, some enjoying this uninvited armed visitation more than three times. Intervention? Invasion is the correct word since these victims were, in international law, sovereign independent countries. But the USA was not intervening to rule directly but to defend comprador classes and install client regimes that would oversee the smooth operation and security of the USA's economic interests.

But by the time the USA had started, and turned into routine, its interventions to maintain neo-colonies in Central and South America, another world shattering event had taken place: in 1917, the great October Revolution in Russia had ushered, on to the historical stage, the era of socialism. And so, the USA imperialism which had taken on the neo-colonial form as opposed to the colonial form of the older European powers, did so in the era of socialism and of the national liberation struggles now irrevocably influenced by the October socialist revolution.

However, until the advent of the Second World War, colonialism remained the dominant form of imperialism. With the weakening of the old imperialist powers by the war; the upsurge of national liberation struggles; the resurgent democratic working-class struggles within the old imperialist beast; and the increasing triumph of socialism, the neo-colonial form into which a retreating European imperialism was encasing itself eventually came into ascendancy. The USA, hardly scathed by the war and with far more experience in the new form, gradually assumed the leadership. The USA for instance rushed to bring South-East Asia, Vietnam being the best example of this, under its influence, determined to take over after the French had retreated.

By the end of the sixties, most of the newly independent countries in Asia and Africa had completed the transition from colonies to neo-colonies. A native neo-colonial elite was now flying the flags and managing the armies and the police ready to crush the population, ensuring, by every military and political trick possible, the stability necessary for the continued Western control of the economy while loudly claiming their non-alignment in international affairs. The USA had become the main guardian of the neo-colonial regimes, arming their military; ensuring the continued flow of western financial aid packages; and often ready to intervene, directly or indirectly, through one of the former European colonial powers, to prop up a threatened regime. Over the years, the USA became the main agency for the destabilisation of any country in Asia and Africa and South America that leaned a bit too heavily on the side of social change; or that wanted to break the neo-colonial chains around its economy, politics and culture. The USA was not even shy of direct invasions as in the case of Grenada in the eighties. But its main means of destabilisation in the countries leaning towards fundamental social change was the creation, followed up by active support, of fake freedom fighters like the Nicaraguan Contras and Angolan Unita. Today the US military bases are everywhere in Asia, Africa and South America, the areas that used to be the sole domain of European capital.

But despite these glaring realities, the two features of modern imperialism – the neo-colonial form and the USA factor – are not often sufficiently at the forefront of the consciousness of those engaged in the anti-imperialist struggles today. These two features are not part of the general mass consciousness in the same way that colonialism and the leadership of the old European oppressor nations used to be perceived and hence successfully fought out. Neo-colonialism and the US leadership of it do not evoke the same sense of horror as the old colonialism and the oppressor nations of Europe used to evoke in the general imagination and in political practice. In some quarters the USA is not even seen as an imperialist power.

All this is partly due to the success of the cultural aspect of modern imperialism. Cultural control today has blunted perceptions and more so the feelings about those perceptions. Cultural control? But we are no longer in the days of the French policies of assimilation or of the British educational policies of creating a compliant native middle class. The USA is not in such direct management of any of these territories as to control and influence cultural policies and practices. We may concede indirect or even direct economic control, but cultural control?

In fact even where neo-colonialism and the USA and the dominant role of the USA are recognised, a lot of literature is devoted to the economic and political aspects of modern imperialism to the almost total exclusion of the cultural factor. Where the cultural factor is taken into account, it is often relegated to the outer edges of the assumed real concerns: the economic and the political. This is partly because the areas of culture and psychology are not as easily quantifiable as the areas of economy and politics. But it is also due to the failure to recognise the integrated and dialectical character of the various aspects that make up the totality of modern imperialism.

It is of course true that imperialism, in whatever form and guise, aims at the complete ownership, management and control of the entire system of production, exchange and distribution of the wealth in its home base and those of other nations and territories. This was perfectly clear in the old colonial system. The bourgeoisie of the oppressor nations of Europe hardly disguised the fact that they were on a mission of economic plunder. Today, US finance capital and the USA-based transnationals are equally on a mission of economic robbery and theft of the resources, the labour, and the produce of the entire 'Third' World. The nations of Asia, Africa and South America are bleeding under the weight of unpayable debts. A traveller in any one of the tri-continental countries will find the same familiar names: IMF; World Bank; General Motors, Firestone, Del Monte, Coca-Cola, MacDonalds etc; Esso, Caltex, Mobil oil, etc; Hilton, Sheraton, etc; and of course other similarly familiar signs from Japan and Western Europe. In short the same tiny group of financial, industrial and commercial interests from the USA and the West generally still control the economies of the various 'Third' World countries.

The economic goes hand in hand with political control. Under colonialism political control was often direct through the settler representatives or through a white-controlled native administration; and of course through the colonial army and police forces. Under the neo-colonial form, control is exercised through a comprador bourgeoisie. Under the USA's leading role in the management of the neo-colonial system, this takes the particular form of erecting and supporting the most reactionary and the most repressive civil or military dictatorships in the world – Pinochet's Chile, Somoza's Nicaragua, Marcos' Philippines, South Korea, Kenya, El Salvador, etc are just a few examples – for as long as they guarantee the continued dominance of USA interests.

The entire economic and political control is effectively facilitated by the cultural factor. In any case, economic and political control inevitably leads to cultural dominance and this in turn deepens that control. The maintenance, management, manipulation, and mobilisation of the entire system of education, language and language use, literature, religion, the media, have always ensured for the oppressor nation power over the transmission of a certain ideology, set of values, outlook, attitudes, feelings etc, and hence power over the whole area of consciousness. This in turn leads to the control of the individual and collective self-image of the dominated nation and classes as well as their image of the dominating nations and classes.

By thus controlling the cultural and psychological domain, the oppressor nation and classes try to ensure the situation of a slave who takes it that to be a slave is the normal human condition. If the exploited and the oppressed of the earth can view themselves and their place in the universe as they are viewed by the imperialist bourgeoisie, then they can become their own policemen, no longer able to see any significant contradiction between their own condition and that of the oppressor nations and classes.

In the era of classical colonialism, this mental control was effected through the confined walls of the colonial school. But generally there was a systematic assault on peoples' languages, literature, dances, names, history, skin colour, religions, indeed their every tool of self definition. In their place were imposed the languages, literatures, religions, names, histories of the colonising nations and classes. Fortunately the colonial school and the churches could not take in the whole population. So only a tiny elite was educated into the culture, values, outlook, and consciousness of the imperialist bourgeoisie. Some even revolted and joined the masses, utilising their very knowledge of the culture of the oppressor to map out strategies and tactics for national self-survival.

This thoroughly colonised petty bourgeoisie was the class that inherited the management of the colonial state under new flags raised aloft at independence. It received almost completely intact the colonial army, the police, the administrative structures and personnel, the judiciary, and of course the entire prison system as developed and refined by colonialism. Their mission became that of overseeing the continuity of the colonial state in a new guise, the neo-colonial guise. They are able to carry out their mission with absolute conviction because they have inherited the same world outlook, even *vis-à-vis* themselves, formerly held by the imperialist bourgeoisie. This is seen for instance in Africa where in a neo-colonial regime the same old disregard of African lives continue. In fact under neo-colonialism, the cultural and the psychological aspects of imperialism become even more important as instruments of mental and spiritual coercion.

Today the USA and the West in general control nearly all the news to and from Third World countries. By that fact alone, they determine how those countries will see themselves in the media. The whole area of news-gathering, the selection of the facts and the angle of viewing them is so important to the USA that when UNESCO persisted in insisting on a new international information order, the USA withdrew its financial dues and summoned Britain to follow suit. The same pattern of control extends to the cinema, television, the video, and the radio. Most of the images on the cinema and television screens of the Third World are actually manufactured in the USA. This dominance is likely to continue with the vast US investment in information technology. With the satellite TV, Cable TV, and the USA-based video productions, these images 'made in the USA' will be received directly by many Third World families. We have already seen the devastating use of this technology in religious propaganda by the USA-based millionaire foundations who now promote idiotic illusions about the pleasures of the heaven to come on a mass hypnotic scale. Even such publicly discredited characters as Swaggert and Oral Roberts will occupy regular spots running into hours of prime television time in a number of African and Third World countries. Jesus-is-my-personal-saviour religions will spread on a mass scale through cassettes, glossy leaflets, and videos.

The USA and the West control the production, training and even the placement of most Third World intellectuals. A good number become trained and cultured into drawing pictures of the world in harmony with the needs of US imperialism. Book and magazine production and distribution is dominated by the USA and the West so that what people in the Third World read is largely determined in the major capitals of the West. In short, the USA and the West control the whole area of the production and dissemination of ideas so basic to cultural determination and the shaping of outlooks on life and social struggles.

Throughout all the above, the Third World is being trained to feel completely at home with the ruling-class values of the US-imperialist bourgeoisie. After a time, any other articulated world view may sound very strange and unreal in the ears of the political believers. With the advent of transnationals the world is finally being made in the image of the West.

The 1990s is going to see at least three centres of imperialism, and possibly rival imperialisms. Western Europe will become united as one centre: this centre will try to bring its spheres of influence in the Third World under the direct European wing. This will mean mainly Africa where British and French interests still predominate. These two nations for instance still maintain sizeable armies in their former colonies. Secondly, there is the Japanese centre with its sphere of economic influence in South-East Asia. And finally of course the North American centre, meaning mainly the USA. This will try to hold on to its leadership of the entire imperialist camp; but the three centres could well see greater inter-imperialist rivalry. Kwame Nkrumah once described neo-colonialism as the last stage of imperialism. How prophetic he was may well be proven by world events in the 1990s, and particularly the incorporation of Eastern Europe into junior membership of the West. The 1990s will see the neo-colonialist form of imperialism entering its last but desperate period especially in the face of intensified national liberation assertions and the increasing demands for fundamental social change. The theatre of struggle will still be in the 'Third' World.

The 1990s will therefore see even greater battles for the control of the minds and hearts of the exploited and the oppressed of the world, trying to mould them in the image of the neo-colonial father in the American heaven. The aim will still be what it has always been: to divide, weaken and scatter resistance. For how a people view themselves will affect how they view their values, their culture, their politics, their economics, and ultimately their relationship to nature and to the entire universe.

An oppressed class, or nation, that believes in itself, in its history, in its destiny, in its capacity to change the scheme of things, will obviously be the stronger in its class and national struggles for political and economic survival. Similarly an oppressed class or nation that loses faith and belief in itself, in its history, in its capacity to change the scheme of things, becomes weakened in its political and economic struggles for survival. Such a class or nation can only work out its destiny within the boundaries clearly drawn by the dominating class and nation.

Fortunately things will never go the way intended by the oppressor for the simple reason that the dominated have always resisted and will always resist. In fact imperialism would never have taken so much trouble to invest so heavily in its repressive machinery or in cultural engineering if the exploited and the oppressed had themselves merely succumbed to their economic fate of forever being the unquestioning drawers and hewers of wood.

In the particular case of Africa, people struggled against the slave trade and slavery; against the colonial invasions and occupations by forces armed with the latest technologies; and today they continue that titanic struggle against neo-colonial encirclement. Between the fifteenth and nineteenth centuries, African people fought wars to preserve their independence against the various invasions from Europe. Under the colonial phase they fought wars for national independence. Today Africa is still engaged in wars to complete the national democratic revolutions as the very first and necessary step towards social change. And in all these phases, the struggle to bring about people's power, social change, a new society is still continuing with even greater intensity as imperialism and its internal class allies in Africa put up barrier after barrier.

In all these struggles, the cultural and intellectual worker has always played an important role. Intellectual workers can draw pictures of the world in harmony with the needs of the forces of human destruction; or in harmony with the forces or resistance for human survival, creativity and renewal. Intellectuals can draw pictures of the universe and its workings to instil fear, despondence, and self-doubt in the oppressed while legitimising the world of the oppressor nations and classes as the norm; or they can draw pictures that instil clarity, strength, hope, to the struggles of the exploited and the oppressed to realise their visions of a new tomorrow.

The 'Third' World that is entering the 1990s can be divided into four main areas corresponding to the four stages in the development of a revolutionary process for fundamental social change.

First, there are those countries which are still under some kind of colonial occupation. These are few in number. Direct occupation of a colonial type is increasingly a thing of the past. It is too obvious and too costly for the occupying forces. These colonial types are opposed by liberation movements.

Then there are the neo-colonies. These are nominally independent with comprador-type regimes running the economy, politics, and culture of the country consistently on behalf of the West. Such neo-colonial regimes also invariably harbour Western military personnel, bases and facilities. In these countries there are movements, people-based movements, spearheading the struggle for democracy and social change.

A third group of countries lean towards social change. They are genuinely trying to safeguard a people-based democracy and to preserve their national independence. Such countries are constantly under threats of destabilisation.

And lastly, there are those countries which have already crossed into the socialist path of development and which once again face imperialist encirclement and economic strangulation. Cuba, for instance, has been facing an economic blockade. Should its economy fail we shall be told that this is because of socialism.

The 'Third' World struggles against imperialism in its neo-colonial form will be the stronger if always linked to the overall international struggle for a new world. Imperialism is a three-headed monster with one head spitting or threatening to spit fire at the socialist world; the other head is spitting fire at the working people in its own home base; and the third head is directing fire and brimstone at the national liberation struggles in the 'Third' World that seem committed to fundamental social change.

It is in the interests of 'Third' World peoples to support the democratic struggles in the USA, Japan, and Western Europe such as the anti-racist groupings, the womens' movements for equality, the workers' struggles, the peace and the environmentalist movements. These democratic movements in the West in turn have to see that the fate of the values they stand for is linked with the success or failure of the national democratic struggles for real liberation in the 'Third' World. They must, out of their own interests, actively intensify their support for anti-neo-colonial democracies and movements in Asia, Africa, and South America. This means, at the very least, opposing their own government's support for dictatorships and tyrannies of various kinds in the 'Third' World. They should also oppose their government's eagerness to send troops to AASA countries when these regimes are threatened by popular forces.

But for the 'Third' World peoples an even more important requirement is the linkages of their struggles. In this respect the notion of south/south dialogue should go beyond the level of sentiment and wishes. Economic exchanges and co-operation can strengthen the links that bind. But quite as important as political dialogues and economic exchange is the cultural factor. The literatures of 'Third' World peoples of Asia, Africa and South America for instance have a lot to learn from each other. Cultural exchanges at the people to people and at institutional levels are vital. This culture is not in contradiction with the democratic tradition in the literatures and cultures of the Western peoples. I am thinking of a tripartite cultural dialogue and exchange between the people of Asia, Africa and South America, on the one hand, and between the peoples of AASA and those of the West, on the other. For quite apart from anything else there are now millions of AASA peoples in the West and they are contributing to the democratic culture of struggle in the West.

The resistance of 'Third' World peoples – mostly of AASA – is a continuing process and it is a struggle against imperialism in whatever form and guise, colonial, neo-colonial, USA-backed or otherwise. For this resistance to be successful it has to be waged at all the levels we have been talking about: economic, political, cultural and psychological. In other words the success of the entire process will be judged finally on how far the economy, politics, culture, indeed the humanity of the peoples of AASA have been liberated. For we are talking about nothing less than the right of all the peoples of the earth to be human. Culture, freed from all the structures of subjugation, national and international, is the best measure of this humanity.

Culture in other words is not something extra, like say a sixth finger on a human hand. Culture has rightly been said to be to society what a flower is to a plant. What is important about a flower is not just its beauty. A flower is the carrier of the seeds for new plants, the bearer of the future of that species of plants. If economic and political liberation are essential for our liberation, equally the liberation of our cultures, our feelings, values, outlook, are a necessary measure of the true extent of that economic and political liberation. Or put it another way: if culture is the product of the totality and continuity of our economic and political struggles, it is also a contributor, a reflection, and a measure of the success of those struggles.

The cultural and the psychological aspects of the continuing resistance against imperialism in the 1990s are an integral part of the overall struggle. Should we ignore the cultural aspects of both imperialism and the resistance against it, we shall merely have scotched the snake not killed it. Imperialism is an integral whole and the struggle against it must also be an integral whole countering, blow for blow, all the areas of its aggression – economic, political, cultural and psychological – with a people-based economy, politics and culture, in the hope of ending up with a liberated people's consciousness and creativity.

Then the positive in each of our cultures would form a foundation for a shared set of human values and heritage on a global scale. The collapse of neo-colonialism and all the international and national structures of domination, dependencies, parasitisms, (Nkrumah's last stage of imperialism), would see the birth of a new world, the beginnings of a truly universal human culture.

II

Freeing Culture from Colonial Legacies

7 The Writer in a Neo-colonial State

The African writer who emerged after the Second World War has gone through three decisive decades which also mark three nodal stages in his growth. He has gone, as it were, through three ages within only the last thirty years or so: the age of the anti-colonial struggle; the age of independence; and the age of neo-colonialism.

First was the fifties, the decade of the high noon of the African people's anti-colonial struggles for full independence. The decade was heralded, internationally, by the triumph of the Chinese Revolution in 1949 and by the independence of India in 1947. It was the decade of the Korean revolution, the Vietnamese defeat of the French at Dien Bien Phu, the Cuban people's ouster of Batista, the stirrings of heroic independence and liberation movements in Asia, the Caribbean and Latin America. In Africa the decade saw the Nasserite national assertion in Egypt culminating in the triumphant nationalisation of the Suez Canal, armed struggles by the Kenya Land and Freedom Army, Mau Mau, against British colonialism and by FLN against French colonialism in Algeria, as well as intensified resistance against the South African Apartheid regime, a resistance it responded to with the Sharpeville massacre. What marks the decade in the popular imagination, however, was the independence of Ghana in 1957 and of Nigeria in 1960 with the promise of more to follow. In Europe, the immediate post-war decades, particularly the fifties, saw consolidation of socialist gains in Eastern Europe and important social-democratic gains in the West. In the USA, the fifties saw an upsurge of civil rights struggles spearheaded by Afro-American people.

It was, in other words, the decade of tremendous anti-imperialist and anti-colonial revolutionary upheavals occasioned by the forcible intervention of the masses in history. It was a decade of hope, the people looking forward to a bright morrow in a new Africa finally freed from colonialism. Kwame Nkrumah was the single most important theoretician and spokesman of this decade. *Towards Colonial Freedom*: that was in fact the title of the book Kwame Nkrumah had published at the beginning of the fifties. How sweet it must have sounded in the ears of all those who dreamt about a new tomorrow! His Ghana became the revolutionary Mecca of the entire anti-colonial movement in Africa. Hutchison, a South African nationalist, captured Ghana's centrality to the era when he called his book – itself an account of his own life and escape from South Africa – simply, *Road to Ghana*. All the continent's nationalist roads of the fifties led to Kwame Nkrumah's Ghana. Everywhere on the continent, the former colonial slave was breaking his chains, and singing songs of hope for a more egalitarian society in its economic, political and cultural life and Nkrumah's Ghana seemed to hold the torch to that life!

The African writer we are talking about was born on the crest of this anti-colonial upheaval and worldwide revolutionary ferment. The anti-imperialist energy and optimism of the masses found its way into the writing of the period. The very fact of his birth was itself evidence of this new assertive Africa. The writing itself, whether in poetry, drama or fiction, even where it was explanatory in intention, was assertive in tone. It was Africa explaining itself, speaking for itself and interpreting its past. It was an Africa rejecting the images of its past as drawn by the artists of imperialism. The writer even flaunted his right to use the language of the former colonial master anyway he liked. No apologies. No begging. The Caliban of the colonial world had been given European languages and he was going to use them even to subvert the master.

There is a kind of self-assuredness, a confidence, if you like, in the scope and mastery of material in some of the best and most representative products of the period: Chinua Achebe's *Things Fall Apart*, Wole Soyinka's *A Dance of the Forests*, Camara Laye's *The African Child*, and Sembene Ousmane's *God's Bits of Wood*. The decade, in politics and in literature, was however best summed up in the very title of Peter Abraham's autobiography, *Tell Freedom*, while the optimism is all there in David Diop's poem 'Africa'.

61

After evoking an Africa of freedom lost as well as the Africa of the current colonialism, he looks to the future with unqualified, total confidence:

Africa tell me Africa
Is this you this back that is bent
This back that breaks under the weight of humiliation
This back trembling with red scars
And saying yes to the whip under the midday sun
But a grave voice answers me
Impetuous son that tree young and strong
That tree there
In splendid loneliness amidst white and faded flowers
That is Africa your Africa
That grows again patiently obstinately
And its fruit gradually acquires
The bitter taste of liberty.

The writer and his work were products of the African revolution even as the writer and the literature tried to understand, reflect, and interpret that revolution. The promptings of his imagination sprang from the fountain of the African anti-imperialist, anti-colonial movement of the forties and fifties. From every tongue came the same tune: Tell Freedom.

But very often the writer who sang 'Tell Freedom' in tune and time with the deepest aspirations of his society did not always understand the true dimensions of those aspirations, or rather he did not always adequately evaluate the real enemy of these aspirations. Imperialism was far too easily seen in terms of the skin pigmentation of the coloniser. It is not surprising of course that such an equation should have been made since racism and the tight caste system in colonialism had ensured that social rewards and punishments were carefully structured on the mystique of colour. *Labour* was not just *labour* but *black labour: capital* was not just *capital* but *white-owned capital*. Exploitation and its necessary consequence, oppression, were black. The vocabulary by which the conflict between colonial labour and imperialist capital was perceived and ideologically fought out consisted of white and black images, sometimes freely interchangeable with the terms 'European' and 'African'. The sentence or phrase was '. . . *when the white-man came to Africa . . .*' and not '. . . *when the imperialist, or the colonialist, came to Africa . . .*', or '. . . *one day these whites will go . . .*' and not '. . . *one day imperialism, or these imperialists, will go . . .*'! Except in a few cases, what was being celebrated in the writing was the departure of the whiteman with the implied hope that the incoming blackman by virtue of his blackness would right the wrongs and heal the wounds of centuries of slavery and colonialism. Were there classes in Africa? No! cried the nationalist politician, and the writer seemed to echo him. The writer could not see the class forces born but stunted in a racially demarcated Africa.

As a result of this reductionism to the polarities of colour and race, the struggle of African people against European colonialism was seen in terms of a conflict of values between the African and the European ways of perceiving and reacting to reality. But which African values? Which European values? Which Black values? Which White values? The values of the European proletariat and of the African proletariat? Of the European imperialist bourgeoisie and of the collaborationist African petty bourgeoisie? The values of the African peasant and those of the European peasant? An undifferentiated uniformity of European, or white, values was posited against an equally undifferentiated uniformity of African, or black, values.

This uniformity of African values was often captured in the realm of political parlance by the grandiloquent phrase, African socialism. The phrase was to be given even greater intellectual sophistication by Julius Nyerere (whose personal integrity has never been in any doubt) when in his famous paper 'Ujamaa: the basis of African socialism' he defined socialism as an attitude of mind. A millionaire (while remaining a millionaire I presume) could be a socialist, and a worker (while remaining a worker) could be a capitalist. Socialism (and therefore its opposite, imperialist capitalism) was reduced to a matter of beliefs, moral absolutes, and not that of a historically changing economic, political and cultural practice. Values without the economic, political and cultural practice that gives rise to them even as they in turn reflect that practice were seen as racially inherent in a people.

In short the writer and the literature he produced did not often take and hence treat imperialism and the class forces it generated as an integrated economic, political and cultural system whose negation and the class struggles this generated had also to be an integrated economic, political and cultural system of its opposite: national independence, democracy and socialism.

And so the writer, armed with an inadequate grasp of the extent, the nature and the power of the enemy and of all the class forces at work could only be shocked by the broken promises as his society entered the second decade.

The beginning of the sixties saw an acceleration of the independence movements. Tanzania, Uganda, Zaire, Kenya, Zambia, Malawi, Congo (Brazzaville), Senegal, Ivory Coast, Mali: country after country won the right to fly a national flag and to sing a national anthem. At the end of the sixties only a few smudges on the map represented old colonies. The OAU was the symbol of the new age, or rather it was the promise of greater unity to come. But if the sixties was the decade of African independence, it was also the decade when old style imperialism tried to halt the momentum of the anti-colonial struggles and the successes of the fifties. Old style imperialism tried to make a last stand. Thus Portuguese colonialism clung tenaciously to Angola, Guinea-Bissau and Mozambique. In Zimbabwe, Ian Smith and his Rhodesian Front, with the active covert and overt encouragement of the big imperialist bourgeoisie, tried to create a second South Africa by means of an American-sounding Unilateral Declaration of Independence (UDI). Internationally – that is, outside of Africa – this last stand of old style imperialism was represented by the USA in South Vietnam. But US domination of South Vietnam also represented new style imperialism; that is US-led imperialism ruling through puppet regimes. Thus in Vietnam lay a clue as to what was happening to the Africa of the sixties, happening that is, to its independence from classical colonialism. New style imperialism was dependent on the 'maturing' of a class of natives, already conceived and born by colonialism, whose positions and aspirations as a group were not in any fundamental conflict with the money-juggling classes, the financial gnomes of the real centres of power like Zurich, the City of London and Wall Street. There is a Kikuyu word, *Nyabaara*, derived from Kiswahili *Mnyapala* which adequately describes these mediators between the imperialist bourgeoisie and the mass of workers and peasants in the former colonies. George Lamming in his novel, *In the Castle of My Skin*, had called it an overseer class. The Boer racist South African regime, not to be outdone, was to caricature the new process when they too went ahead to create their own Bantustans. Bantustanism! How innovative the Boers are! But in a sense, how true!

To the majority of African people in the new states, independence did not bring about fundamental changes. It was independence with the ruler holding a begging bowl and the ruled holding a shrinking belly. It was independence with a question mark. The age of independence had produced a new class and a new leadership that often was not very different from the old one. Black skins, white masks? White skins, black masks? Black skins concealing colonial settlers' hearts? In each of the African languages there was an attempt to explain the new phenomenon in terms of the 'White' and 'Black' symbols by which colonialism had been seen and fought out. But really, this was a new company, a company of African profiteers firmly deriving their character, power and inspiration from their guardianship of imperialist interests.

It was Frantz Fanon in his book *Les Damnés de la Terre*, first published in French in 1961 and later (1965) in English under the title *The Wretched of the Earth*, who prophetically summed up the character of this emergent phenomenon. The class that took over power after independence was an underdeveloped middle class which was not interested in putting the national economy on a new footing, but in becoming an intermediary between Western interests and the people, a handsomely paid business agent of the Western bourgeoisie:

Before independence, the leader generally embodies the aspirations of the people for independence, political liberty and national dignity. But as soon as independence is declared, far from embodying in concrete form the needs of the people in what touches bread, land and the restoration of the country to the sacred hands of the people, the leader will reveal his inner purpose: to become the general president of that company of profiteers impatient for their returns which constitutes the national bourgeoisie.

I have always argued that literature written by Africans, and particularly the literature of this period, cannot really be understood without a proper and thorough reading of the chapter 'Pitfalls of National Consciousness' in Fanon's *The Wretched of the Earth*. The literature of this period was really a series of imaginative footnotes to Frantz Fanon.

The new regimes in the independent states increasingly came under pressure from external and internal sources. The external pressure emanated from the West who wanted these states to maintain their independence and non-alignment firmly on the side of Western economic and political interests. Where a regime showed a consistent desire to break away from the Western orbit, destabilisation through economic sabotage and political intrigue was set in motion. The US role in bringing down Lumumba and installing the Mobutu military regime in Zaire at the very beginning of the decade was a sign of things to come.

The internal pressure came from the people who soon saw that independence had brought no alleviation to their poverty and certainly no end to political repression. People saw in most of the new regimes dependence on foreigners, grand mismanagement and well-maintained police boots. To quote Fanon: 'scandals are numerous, ministers grow rich, their wives doll themselves up, the members of Parliament feather their nests and there is not a soul down to the simple policeman or the customs officer who does not join in the great procession of corruption.'

Some military intervened either at the promptings of the West or in response to what they genuinely saw and felt as the moral decay. But they too did not know what else to do with the state except to run the status quo with the gun held at the ready – not against imperialism – but against the very people the army had ostensibly stepped in to save.

Thus the sixties, the age of independence, became the era of *coups d'état* whether Western-backed or in patriotic response to internal pressures. Zaire in 1960 and 1965; Nigeria and Ghana in 1966; Sierra Leone, Sudan, Mali, Uganda: all these and more fell to the armies and by 1970 virtually every independent state had experienced a measure of military coups, attempted coups or threats of coups. The result was often intra-class fratricide as in the case of Zaire and Nigeria but one that dragged the masses into meaningless deaths, starvation and stagnation. Wars initiated by Nyabaaras! The era of *coups d'état* also threw up two hideous monstrosities: Bokassa and Idi Amin, two initial darlings of the West, who were to make a total mockery of the notion of independence, but who also, in those very actions, made a truthful expression of that kind of independence. Hideous as they were, they were only symbols of all the broken promises of independence.

What was wrong with Africa? What had gone wrong? The mood of disillusionment engulfed the writer and the literature of the period. It was Chinua Achebe in *A Man of the People* who correctly reflected the conditions that bred coups and rumours of coups.

The fictional narrator captures in the image of a house the deliberate murder of democracy by the new leadership:

We had all been in the rain together until yesterday. Then a handful of us – the smart and the lucky and hardly ever the best – had scrambled for the one shelter our former rulers left, and had taken it over and barricaded themselves in. And from within they sought to persuade the rest through numerous loudspeakers, that the first phase of the struggle had been won and that the next phase – the extension of our house – was even more important and called for new and original tactics; it required that all argument should cease and the whole people speak with one voice and that any more dissent and argument outside the door of the shelter would subvert and break down the whole house.

A Man of the People, coming out at about the same time as the first Nigerian military coup, had shown that a writer could be a prophet. But other writings – particularly Ayi Kwei Armah's *The Beautyful Ones Are Not Yet Born*, and Okot p'Bitek's *Song of Lawino* – were equally incisive in their horror at the moral decay in the new states. The writer responded to the decay by appealing to the conscience of the new class. If only they would listen! If only they would see the error of their ways! He pleaded, lamented, threatened, painted the picture of the disaster ahead, talked of a fire next time. He tried the corrective antidote of contemptuous laughter, ridicule, direct abuse with images of shit and urine, every filth imaginable. The writer often fell back upon the kind of revenge Marx once saw the

67

progressive elements among the feudal aristocracy taking against the new bourgeoisie that was becoming the dominant class in nineteenth century Europe. They, the aristocracy, 'took their revenge by singing lampoons on their new master, and whispering in his ears sinister prophecies of coming catastrophe'.

> In this way arose feudal socialism; half lamentation, half lampoon; half echo of the past, half menace of the future; at times, by its bitter, witty and incisive criticism, striking the bourgeoisie to the very heart's core but always ludicrous in its effect, through total incapacity to comprehend the march of history.
>
> *The Communist Manifesto*

Thus the writer in this period was still limited by his inadequate grasp of the full dimension of what was really happening in the sixties: the international and national realignment of class forces and class alliances. What the writer often reacted to was the visible lack of moral fibre of the new leadership and not necessarily the structural basis of that lack of a national moral fibre. Sometimes the writer blamed the people – the recipients of crimes – as well as the perpetrators of the crimes against the people. At times the moral horror was couched in terms perilously close to blaming it all on the biological character of the people. Thus although the literature produced was incisive in its observation, it was nevertheless characterised by a sense of despair. The writer in this period often retreated into individualism, cynicism, or into empty moral appeals for a change of heart.

It was the third period, the seventies, that was to reveal what really had been happening in the sixties: the transition of imperialism from the colonial to the neo-colonial stage. On the international level, the US-engineered overthrow of the Allende regime in Chile showed the face of victorious neo-colonialism. The decade saw the clear ascendancy of US-dominated transnational financial and industrial monopolies in most of Asia, Africa and Latin America. This ascendancy was to be symbolised by the dominance of the IMF and the World Bank in the determination of the economies and hence the politics and culture of the affected countries in Asia, Africa and Latin America. The era saw the USA surround Africa with military bases or with some kind of direct US military presence all the way from Morocco via Diego Garcia to Kenya, Egypt and of course the Mediterranean Sea. The aims of the Rapid Deployment Forces formed in the same decade were unashamedly stated as interventionist in Third World affairs, i.e. in affairs of the neo-colonies. Indeed, the decade saw an increasing readiness of former colonial powers to enter Africa militarily without even a trace of shame. The increasingly open, naked financial, industrial (e.g. Free Trade Zones etc), military and political interference of Western interests in the affairs of African countries with the active co-operation of the ruling regimes in the same countries, showed quite clearly that the so-called independence had only opened each of the African countries to wider imperialist interests. Dependence abroad, repression at home, became the national motto.

But if the seventies revealed more clearly the neo-colonial character of many of the African countries, the seventies also saw very important and eye-opening gains by the anti-imperialist struggles. Internationally (outside Africa), the single most important event was the defeat of the USA in Vietnam. But there were other shattering blows against neo-colonialism: Nicaragua and Iran, for instance.

In Africa, the seventies saw a victorious resurgence of anti-imperialism. The armed struggles in Angola, Mozambique, Guinea-Bissau and Zimbabwe had clearly gained from errors of the earlier anti-colonial movements in the fifties. They could see the enemy much more clearly and they could clearly analyse their struggles in terms that went beyond just the question of colour and race. Their enemy was imperialism and the classes that allied with imperialism. Within the independent African countries, *coups d'état* began to take on a more anti-imperialist and anti-neo-colonial character.

Although occurring in 1981 and 1983 respectively, Rawlings' coup in Ghana and Sankara's in Burkina Faso (previously Upper Volta) are the better examples of this tendency. But a more telling symbol was the emergence in the seventies of a people-based guerrilla movement fighting for a second independence. The armed liberation guerrilla movements in places like Uganda and Zaire may well come to stand to neo-colonialism what Kenya Land and Freedom Army and FLN in Algeria stood to colonialism in the fifties. The phenomenon of university-educated youth and secondary school graduates opting to join workers and peasants in the bush to fight on a clear programme of a national democratic revolution as a first and necessary stage for a socialist transformation is something new in the Africa of the seventies. Whatever their ultimate destiny, these post-colonial guerrilla movements certainly symbolise the convergence of the worker's hammer and the peasant's machete or jembe with the pen and the gun.

The awakening to the realities of imperialism was reflected in some very important theoretical political breakthroughs in the works of Amilcar Cabral, Walter Rodney, Samir Amin, Dan Nabudere, Bala Mohamed, Nzongola-Ntalaja and in many papers emanating from university centres in many parts of the continent. Imperialism was becoming a subject of serious and even passionate academic debate and scholarly dissertations. The Dar es Salaam debate, now published as *Debate on Class, State and Imperialism*, stands out. But other places like Ahmadu Bello University and Ife University in Nigeria, Nairobi University in Kenya, and the Universities of Cape Coast and Ghana were emerging as centres of progressive thought; but even outside the university campuses, progressive debate was raging and it is not an accident that the *Journal of African Marxists* should emerge in the seventies.

Once again this new anti-imperialist resurgence was reflected in literature. For the writer from Mozambique, Angola, Guinea Bissau, his content and imagery were clearly derived from the active struggles of the people. Even in the countries that became independent in the fifties and the sixties, the writer started taking a more and more critical stand against the anti-national, anti-democratic, neo-colonial character of the ruling regimes. He began to connect these ills not just to the moral failings or otherwise of this or that ruler, but to the perpetuation of imperialist domination through the comprador ruling classes in Africa.

The writer in the seventies gradually began to take imperialism seriously. He was also against the internal classes, those new companies of profiteers that allied with imperialism. But the writer tried to go beyond just explanation and condemnation. One can sense in some of the writing of this period an edging towards the people and a search for new directions. The writer in the seventies was coming face to face with neo-colonialism. He was really a writer in a neo-colonial state. Further he was beginning to take sides with the people in the class struggle in Africa.

The writer who edged towards the people was caught in various contradictions. Where, for instance, did he stand in relation to the neo-colonial state in which he was a citizen, and within which he was trying to function?

A neo-colonial regime is, by its very character, a repressive machine. Its very being, in its refusal to break with the international and national structures of exploitation, inequality and oppression, gradually isolates it from the people. Its real power base resides not in the people but in imperialism and in the police and the army. To maintain itself it shuts all venues of democratic expression. It, for instance, resorts to one-party rule, and since in effect the party is just a bureaucratic shell, this means resorting to one man rule, despotism à la Marquez's novel, *The Autumn of the Patriarch!* All democratic organisations are outlawed or else brought under the ruler, in which case they are emptied of any democratic life. Why then should the regime allow any democracy in the area of culture? Any democratic expression in the area of culture becomes a threat to such a regime's very peculiar brand of culture: the culture of silence and fear run and directed from police cells and torture chambers.

The Kenya that emerged from the seventies is a good illustration of the workings of a neo-colonial state. At the beginning of the decade Kenya was a fairly 'open society' in the sense that Kenyans could still debate issues without fear of prison. But as the ruling party under Kenyatta, and later under Moi, continued cementing the neo-colonial links to the West, the Kenya regime became more and more intolerant of any views that questioned neo-colonialism. In the fifties, Kenyans had fought to get rid of *all* foreign military presence from her soil. In 1980 the Kenyan authorities had given military base facilities to the USA. The matter was not even debated in Parliament. Kenyans learnt about it through debates in the US Congress. Now within the same decade which saw the Kenyan coast turned over for use by the US military machine, the Kenya regime had banned all centres of democratic debate. Even the university was not spared. University lecturers were imprisoned or detained

71

without trial; among them were writers like Al Amin Mazrui and Edward Oyugi.

Another lecturer, but also a writer and Kenya's foremost national historian, Maina wa Kĩnyattĩ, has served a prison sentence in a maximum security prison for doing intensive work on Mau Mau. Maina wa Kĩnyattĩ was educated in Kenya and in the United States of America. On returning to Kenya at the beginning of the seventies, he joined the History Department at Kenyatta University College. He became very concerned that ten years after the Kenya Land and Freedom Army had forced colonialism to retreat and allow Kenya a measure of self-rule and independence, no work had been done by Kenyan scholars on the actual history and literature of those who died that Kenya might be free. He set about collecting the songs and poems of the Mau Mau era, some of which he later edited into a book: *Thunder From the Mountain: Mau Mau Patriotic Songs*. He also started work on the whole anti-colonial resistance within the context of the Kenyan history of struggle from the nineteenth to twentieth centuries. The result? He languished in jail, going blind.*

Over the same decade, the regime became very intolerant of theatre and any cultural expression that sided with the people. Kamĩrĩĩthũ Community Education and Cultural Centre's Open Air Theatre was razed to the ground. A number of plays were stopped. Kenyan writers like Mĩcere Mũgo, Ngũgĩ wa Mĩriĩ, Kĩmani Gecau, were forced into exile. In February 1985, the regime climaxed its decade of intolerance by bludgeoning 12 students to death, and 150 others into hospital; 14† went to jail to join another 10 serving long jail terms of up to 10 years. Five others, were tortured and subsequently sentenced from 6 to 12 months in jail for holding an interdenominational prayer meeting in day time on an open university sports ground.

How does a writer function in such a society? He can of course adopt silence or self-censorship, in which case he ceases to be an effective writer. Or he can become a state functionary, an option some Kenyan writers have now embraced, and once again cease to be an effective writer of the people. Or he may risk jail or exile, in which

*Released October 1989 after 6½ years.
†Released after serving their 6-month term in jail.

case he is driven from the very sources of his inspiration. Write and risk damnation. Avoid damnation and cease to be a writer. That is the lot of the writer in a neo-colonial state.

There are other contradictions of a writer in a neo-colonial state. For whom does he write? For the people? But then what language does he use? It is a fact that the African writers who emerged after the Second World War opted for European languages. All the major African writers wrote in English, French and Portuguese. But by and large, all the peasants and a majority of the workers – the masses – have their own languages.

Isn't the writer perpetuating, at the level of cultural practice, the very neo-colonialism he is condemning at the level of economic and political practice? For whom a writer *writes* is a question which has not been satisfactorily resolved by the writers in a neo-colonial state. For the African writer, the language he has chosen already has chosen his audience.

Whatever the language the writer has opted for, what is his relationship to the content? Does he see reality in its unchangingness or in its changingness? To see reality in stagnation or in circles of the same movements is to succumb to despair. And yet for him to depict reality in its revolutionary transformation from the standpoint of the people – the agents of change – is once again to risk damnation by the state. For a writer who is depicting reality in its revolutionary transformation is, in effect, telling the upholders of the status quo: even this too shall pass away.

I think I have said enough about the writer in the third period – the seventies – to show that his lot, particularly when he may want to edge towards the people, is not easy.

In the world, the struggle between democratic and socialist forces for life and human progress on the one hand, and the imperialist forces for reaction and death on the other is still going on and it is bound to become more fierce. Imperialism is still the enemy of human kind and any blow against imperialism whether in the Philippines, El Salvador, Chile, South Korea is clearly a blow for democracy and change. In Africa, the struggle of the Namibian* people and of South African / Azanian people has intensified. And

*Namibia is now free

73

as the Zimbabwean, Angolan, and Mozambican struggles took the African revolution a stage further than where it had been left by the FLN and the Kenya Land and Freedom Army in the fifties, in the same way the successful outcome of the Namibian and South African peoples' struggle will push the entire continent on to a new stage. In a special way, the liberation of South Africa is the key to the liberation of the entire continent from neo-colonialism.

Within the neo-colonial states, the anti-imperialist alliance of democratic forces will intensify the struggle against the rule of the alliance of the comprador classes and imperialism. There will be more and more anti-imperialist coups of the Sankara type. There will be an increase in the Uganda type anti-neocolonial guerrilla movements. There will be greater and greater call and demand for a Pan-Africanism of the proletariat and the peasantry through their progressive democratic organisation. Each new stage in the struggle for real independence, democracy and socialism will have learnt from the errors of the previous attempts, successes and even failures. We shall see a further heightening of the war against neo-colonialism. For as in the days of colonialism, so now in the days of neo-colonialism, the African people are still struggling for a world in which they can control that which their collective sweat produces, a world in which they will control the economy, politics and culture to make their lives accord with where they want to go and who they want to be.

But as the struggle continues and intensifies, the lot of the writer in a neo-colonial state will become harder and not easier. His choice? It seems to me that the African writer now, the one who opts for becoming an integral part of the African revolution, has no choice but that of aligning himself with the people: their economic, political and cultural struggle for survival. In that situation, he will have to confront the languages spoken by the people in whose service he has put his pen. Such a writer will have to *rediscover* the *real* languages of struggle in the actions and speeches of his people, learn from their great heritage of orature, and above all, learn from their great optimism and faith in the capacity of human beings to remake their world and renew themselves. He must be part of the song the people sing as once again they take up arms to smash the neo-colonial state to complete the anti-imperialist national democratic revolution they had started in the fifties, and even earlier. A people united can never be defeated and the writer must be part and parcel of that revolutionary unity for democracy, socialism and the liberation of the human spirit to become even more human.

8 *Resistance to Damnation*

The Role of Intellectual Workers

The liberation of South Africa is the key to the social liberation of the continent. Even our enemies know this. That is why they so tenaciously hold on to the key with guns and a racist ideology. But even as an adult, my talking about the survival of children is not an act of charity.

Children are the future of any society. If you want to know the future of a society look at the eyes of the children. If you want to maim the future of any society, you simply maim the children. Thus the struggle for the survival of our children is the struggle for the survival of our future. The quantity and quality of that survival is the measurement of the development of our society. Enslave the children and you enslave parents. Enslave the parents and you enslave children. Thus if you enslave children, you are enslaving the survival and development of the entire society – its present and its future. Survival and development are an integrated whole. Survival is the pre-condition of any development. And development is the basis of our continued survival.

Let me very briefly isolate the five crucial elements in that integrated whole: physical survival, economic survival, political survival, cultural survival, and psychological (or identity) survival.

Let us first take physical survival and development. That the precondition of any human development is physical survival is obvious. But it also needs saying. Even a new-born baby has mechanism of self-defence however fragile to ensure its survival. Mother and father will do anything to protect the young first against any harm from nature – diseases, wild animals etc – and from human enemies. We have to *be* in order to *be*!

76

But physical survival is also dependent on food, clothes and shelter. We struggle with nature to procure the basic means of our survival: food, clothes and shelter. We produce the means of our life. Thus we ensure the economic survival, through production and distribution. We need the earth, we need our labour. We need tools. We produce, we create, we survive, we change, we develop.

But this condition of our physical and economic survival need regulation to ensure resolution of conflicts in a manner that would not threaten our survival. A society needs political survival – that is the retention of power in its hands – to regulate the life of that society in a manner beneficial to that society. The question of power, and of who wields this power, and on whose behalf that power is wielded is crucial as a guardian of its physical, and economic survival. The power to decide between options, alternatives, tactics and strategies for survival should be wielded by the society.

And then there is the question of cultural survival: education, languages, art, literature, music, dances. These are evolved in society. What holds that society together is the culture it develops in the course of its struggles for economic and political survival. Thus culture is not an extra growth, like say an extra finger. It is an integral part of our growth. It is a product of our growth. It is what a flower is to a tree. The important thing about a flower, as I have said in another context, is not just its beauty. A flower contains the seeds of the tree's future growth, its survival.

Culture carries the values, ethical, moral and aesthetic by which people conceptualise or see themselves and their place in history and the universe.

These values are the basis of a society's consciousness and outlook, the whole area of a society's make-up, its identity. A sense of belonging, a sense of identity is part of our psychological survival. Colonialism through racism tried to turn us into societies without heads. Racism, whose highest institutionalised form is apartheid, is not an accident. It is an ideology of control through divide and rule, obscurantism, a weakening of resistance through a weakening of a sense of who we are. Thus psychological survival is necessary. We need values that do not distort our identity, our conception of our rightful place in history, in the universe of the natural and human order.

A sense of who we are in turn reacts on our values, on our cultural, political, economic, and physical being. Psychological survival – identity survival – thus reacts on all the other levels of survival. Development is thus an integrated whole. When we talk of survival and development say of a child, we are talking about the development of the whole.

The five levels are true for the child as they are for the adult. Only the child is more vulnerable, at all those levels. A people are truly free when they control all the tools, all the instruments, all the means of their physical, economic, political, cultural and psychological survival. In short, when they control the means and context of their integrated survival and development.

But in the Africa of the twentieth century, or for that matter the Africa of the last 400 years, that free integrated self-development had not been possible, has in fact been brutally prevented. What has threatened, thwarted, and prevented Africa's integrated survival?

First it has been the external factor of foreign invasion, occupation and control and second, the internal factor of collaboration with the external threat. Whether under Western slavery and the slave trade, under colonialism and today under neo-colonialism the two factors have interacted to the detriment of our being. The greedy chief and feudal elements collaborated with the slave dealer from Europe. The same story repeats itself under colonial invasion and occupations. Some greedy chiefs and other elements bred by the new colonial overlords, collaborated with the main external imperialist factor. The story repeats itself, in a more painful way, under neo-colonialism.

This interplay between the external threat and internal collaborator is best seen in South Africa today. But I don't want to be vague about this external factor. For the last 400 years South Africa has been feeding Western Europe. After all, Vasco da Gama landed at the Cape in the fifteenth century. Today South Africa continues to feed and develop Western Europe and the USA. US-based transnationals are the dominant factor in South Africa. Western interests are thus partners in apartheid. South Africa is itself a Frontline State – for Western interests. But that external factor (imperialism) is aided by internal collaborating forces.

Nowhere is this clearer than in Angola and Mozambique. The two states had correctly perceived the Enemy – within and without. The examples of Angola and Mozambique producing integrated development – thus providing an alternative model to the neo-colonial model adopted by many who received their independence in the early sixties – was going to be a real threat to those interests that had for centuries impoverished a continent. MNR and UNITA had to be created. Who supports MNR and UNITA today? Where do they get their diplomatic and material support? I am asking a rhetorical question. An internal collaborating force is being forced on Mozambique and Angola. For a neo-colony cannot be created without such collaborating neo-slave drivers! Imperialism led by USA wants to turn Mozambique and Angola into neo-colonies!

In short, Western interests are behind apartheid which in turn attempts a racist hegemony over Southern Africa. In the process these interests have threatened our physical survival (through killings), our economic survival through land confiscation and the plunder of natural and human resources, or through destabilisation, our political survival through direct brutal occupation or through collaborating elements like MNR/UNITA and our cultural survival and psychological survival through the contol of the *media*, the arts and television. In short through control of the instruments of collective self-definition. Image control: this is the phrase. We have even been stripped of our *names*, and *languages*, the two immediate symbols of the means of self-definition.

I have so far concentrated on the forces threatening our survival, the forces of our exploitation and control. But what of the forces ensuring our survival? They go by the name of **resistance**. What has ensured our survival is because for the last 400 years African people have waged resistance. And this resistance necessarily had to be at all the levels we have been talking about. We have created resistance armies to fight for our physical survival. We have organised in order to seize back the means of our economic survival. We have fought back and organised to seize back the means of our political survival. And we have fought back to seize back the means of our self-definition. This resistance today is being carried to even higher levels by the ANC and all the other progressive liberation forces in South Africa.

The degree, intensity, quality and success of this resistance has always been dependent on how all the five levels have been seen as an integrated whole.

But the success of the resistance is also dependent on an *internal factor* and an *external factor*. Put it this way. The main antagonism today is between imperialist enemy classes and the internal resistance classes. But just as imperialism, the external factor is helped by traitorous internal elements, so the resistance forces need an alliance with external friends of human liberation. Thus imperialism and its internal allies and the national liberation forces and their external allies are the two contending forces in Africa.

Children in Africa best exemplify the struggle between the two contending forces in Africa today: the forces of our demise on the one hand, and the forces of our survival on the other.

The children have been the most vulnerable victim of the forces of our demise. That is very clear. But the children are also part of the **resistance**. Soweto children have become a metaphor of the best and the most heroic in our resistance history. Mozambican children, in their flight and refusal to succumb show we can look to the future with hope. We shall overcome!!

Indeed this **resistance** will eventually succeed. And it will be finally successful when people are in total control of all the means of their physical, economical, political, cultural, psychological and spiritual survival. So we have to strengthen our capacity, and that of our children, to **resist the evil**.

When and where do the arts and artists come into this? From the above analysis it is clear that artists are part of the image-making processes. They draw the pictures of the world. The arts and artists and intellectual workers can draw pictures of the world in harmony with the needs of the forces of human destruction; or in harmony with the forces of resistance and survival. And here there are no neutral images. If you find an MNR bandit cutting the limbs off a child, what neutral song can you sing about it? What neutral image can you draw? What about the picture of the forces supporting MNR or those supporting the child? What neutral song can you sing? What neutral image can you draw; what neutral philosophy can you articulate? Yes, what neutral prayer can you give?

Art and artists can draw pictures of the universe of our struggle that instil strength, clarity, hope, to our struggle to realise visions of a new tomorrow as embodied in the struggle and survival of our children; or pictures that instil fear and despondence or give rational, artistic legitimacy to the world of the oppressor-nations and classes. Artistic and intellectual ideological struggles, are part of the overall struggle for survival and development.

Finally what is to be done? We must not mislead the people as to who the real enemy is! MNR, UNITA, Apartheid, these are particular manifestations of our enemy. But who arms them? For whose benefit? The Western forces behind the Contras in Nicaragua are exactly the same force behind apartheid and the MNR/UNITA banditry.

While the internal resistance factor can confront these forces, the friends and allies of the resistance must bring pressure to bear on those governments that ally with apartheid, the MNR and UNITA. Even within Africa, the neo-colonial regimes that ally with apartheid and harbour spokesmen of MNR and UNITA bandits should be exposed. The democratic struggle in the Western world, the peace movement in the world, the anti-racist movements in the West and the anti-neo-colonial movements in Africa must together support the forces of resistance in Southern Africa. In other words, there should be a two-pronged attack: bring pressure to bear on these governments that collaborate with apartheid; and support every effort of the Frontline States and the liberation forces in South Africa to strengthen their continuing capacity for resistance.

But within our field as artists, writers and intellectuals, let our **Pen, Brushes and Voices** articulate the dreams of all the children of Southern Africa for a world in which their integrated survival and development is ensured. Let us sing songs of the possibility of a new tomorrow, a new world. A luta continua!

9 The Role of the Scholar in the Development of African Literatures

Scholars and works of scholarship have had an important influence on the development of African literatures. Some of the major African writers started off as would-be scholars. They began writing as students or teachers on university campuses or on school compounds. Often their inspiration, at least initially, came from the textbooks they were reading; many of them tried to write stories, poems or plays imitating the styles of their favourite textbooks.

Scholars have also made an impact on these new literatures by commenting on them. Writers have been affected by critical assessments of their work, and so too have readers, whose responses to a book can be conditioned by what they read about it. So the scholar, as a critic, has been in a position to influence the direction of the literature he comments upon. He can play a vital role as an interpreter of African fictions and realities.

The question is, how can he perform his role more effectively? The obvious answer, of course, is that he must always be committed to the truth – that is, be faithful to what he sees, what he hears, what he touches. But how he perceives things will depend on the base from which he operates. The act of seeing can be hampered or limited by the point at which one is located when trying to see. For instance, twenty people sitting around a table in a room will see slightly different things, depending on where they sit in relation to others and to those objects. If these people were to be asked to describe the room, each would strive to express the truth about what he saw, but since all of them would be observing from different angles of vision, they might end up with twenty different descriptions of the same room. And this in turn could lead people outside the room to suspect them of telling lies, for how else could there be so many conflicting stories about the same place?

The base I am talking about need not be a physical locality. It can also be the social base from which one is looking at literary or historical reality. This base too can affect a person's vision and be decisive as to what features are highlighted or not. If one reads commentaries on African literature, for instance, one occasionally will find two critics saying things about a literary work that are totally irreconcilable. If one looks very carefully at their statements, one will discover that the base of their disagreement does not really reside in the text but rather in the social positions from which they are viewing the text.

So let me re-state the two factors that do affect scholars and scholarship: faithfulness to what is being observed; and the social or class base from which the scholar is viewing reality.

But there is a third factor, a very important factor, and that is the attitude of the scholar to that which he has observed from his chosen base. Scholars must always strive to be conscious of the attitude they develop toward the object of their observation. Assuming that they have opted for the kind of social base that will afford them the widest possible angle of vision so that they can see clearly and record clearly, they must still be alert to their attitudes toward that which they are viewing.

Now one thing affecting the development of African literature is imperialism, the most important social force in Africa in this century. But most scholars in African literature have refused to recognise that there is such a force as imperialism. Indeed, if it is discussed at all, usually it is to dismiss it as phrase-mongering work of politicians only. Such literary scholars tend to say, 'Oh, that's politics. That's really not for us.' Scholars in other disciplines – economics and politics, for instance – have long recognised imperialism as a social force in Africa, but literary scholars are suspicious of it. When it creeps into academic studies, they claim that such studies are not really acceptable as literary scholarship but are political scholarship, and so on. Yet imperialism, both in its colonial and neo-colonial stages, is the one force that affects *everything* in Africa – politics, economics, culture, absolutely every aspect of human life. African literature itself has grown and developed in response to imperialism.

One of the most obvious ways in which imperialism has affected the development of African literature is in language choice. During the colonial stage of Western imperialism in Africa, African languages were suppressed and European languages were deliberately given a status that made them the inevitable vehicle of African peoples' self-definition.*

This has resulted in an enormous contradiction. These languages may be the official languages in Africa today but they are not the languages of the majority of people inhabiting Africa. The vast majority in each nationality – that is, the peasants and the workers – still use their own languages. Yet, African writers feel it necessary and natural to write in European languages about African peasants and workers.

Thus, a scholar is immediately confronted with the question of identity: what is African literature? Because today it is generally expected that Africans will write in European languages, my own attempts to write in African languages have prompted interesting reactions from some scholars. People will say, 'Oh, but this literature won't be available to us. Why are you becoming so chauvinistic?' One senses in these remarks the assumption that in writing in an African language one is departing from what is normal and behaving in a manner that is abnormal. In fact, abnormality has been turned into normality. That which is normal in all other civilisations, in all other societies, in all other phases in history is transformed into abnormality. Once reality is perverted so totally, everyone begins to see things upside-down. This topsy-turvy vision has been convenient for 'African' literature scholars who have been spared the necessity of having to learn African languages in order to come to terms with the literature produced and the realities embodied in those languages.

In addition to creating these contradictions and distortions, imperialism has led to the active repression of African literature and to the persecution of writers, artists and scholars in several African countries. During the colonial era, this was a norm. But how does one explain this persecution in the post-colonial era? Basically, it has to do with the class character of the national leadership. The African bourgeoisie that inherited the flag from the departing colonial powers was created within the cultural womb of imperialism. That

*For a fuller discussion of this point, see my book *Decolonising the Mind*.

is, it was a bourgeoisie with a mentality, an outlook, which was in harmony with the outlook of the bourgeoisie in the colonising countries. So even after they inherited the flag, their mental outlook, their attitudes toward their own societies, toward their own history, toward their own languages, toward everything national, tended to be foreign; they saw things through eyeglasses given them by their European bourgeois mentors.

As a consequence, the economic, political and cultural structures of colonialism have more or less remained intact. There has been no dismantling of the colonial state. The result has been the gradual political alienation of the ruling elite in these countries. And the way they have responded to this political alienation has been by repression. They have been making sure that all centres of democratic expression or opposition are crushed, for this is the only way they can maintain themselves in power.

Remember that in this they have not been practising anything new. It has been very much in character with them, who are themselves the products of imperialism, because their image of power derives from the colonial past and their exercise of power is therefore modelled on colonial practices. During the colonial period there was no democracy; there was only repression. So the notion these neo-colonial leaders have of power comes straight from the very womb from which they emerged as a class.

Their repression does not choose only politicians or political activists as targets. When these regimes shut off avenues of democratic expression, they suppress every aspect of life. This is where cultural workers come into the picture. Literature, which often carries within it seeds of revolt and seeds of human affirmation, now comes to be seen as a threat. So after they have suppressed parliament, after they have banned people-based political parties, after they have put opponents of neo-colonialism in jail, why should they give free expression to that other voice, the cultural voice which is articulating the same anti-imperialist position but inbetween hard covers? Why allow that voice to be heard? Why allow it in theatre, in poetry, in song? So cultural activity becomes increasingly a target for wholesale political and military repression.

A good example of this kind of cultural repression can be seen today in Kenya, a country which for a long time was painted as a shining example of stability and democracy in Africa. So great was

Kenya's reputation that when university lecturers, scholars like you and me, were thrown in jail – some of them detained without trial, others put away for ten years for doing no more than discharging what we are now discussing as the responsibilities of the scholar – the international outcry was minimal. These scholars and their students are still in jail today. The majority of Kenya's scholarly community have kept silent in face of this neo-colonial tyranny.

I would have liked to see more scholars, both in and outside the country, particularly those researching on Kenya and on Africa, come out more strongly and more solidly in aid of their colleagues in the jails of the Kenya neo-colonial regime. This is part of their responsibility as scholars. But I have come across some who were more worried about their visas into the country to do research on the Kenyan situation than in expressing even the faintest concern about their counterparts.

In the end everything depends on the attitudes we adopt toward what we see. In terms of the interpretation of literature, we will project our political views on what we read. A scholar or critic who in real life is suspicious of people who fight for liberation will be suspicious of characters in a novel or play who are freedom fighters. His critique of them as characters will be conditioned by how he feels about such people in real life. Similarly, his attitude to the literary depiction of repression and the persecution of progressive writers and scholars, will be in harmony with what he feels about those processes in real life.

My own view is that scholarship will be able to contribute to the development of African literatures only if scholars manage to free themselves from limiting angles of vision. To accomplish this they will have to adopt a social base that enables them to see, hear, smell and taste more accurately. And I would hope that as a result of adopting that kind of social base, they would also form attitudes that would encourage them to raise their voice in real life against the repression of scholars, writers and artists in Africa today, be it in neo-colonies like Kenya or in the older colonies like South Africa and Namibia.

In a situation where one class or nation is sitting on other classes and nations, there are only two types of scholars: those on the side of oppression and those on the side of resistance. Neutrality in such a situation is a myth; or, rather, it means that such a scholar is basically on the side of the bully. Hence the importance of scholars recognising (or refusing to be blind to) the continuing Western imperialist stranglehold on Africa albeit in a neo-colonial form – that is, a form that allows the Western bourgeoisie to continue fattening on Africa's wealth through the political alliance of an armed – mercenary, really – native ruling clique installed and maintained by the West in the first place.

A consistent anti-imperialist position – that is, a position that struggles against or that exposes the continued neo-colonial control of African economics and cultures by the Western bourgeoisie – is the minimum necessary for a committed, responsible scholarship in Africa, or anywhere in the 'Third' World. Certainly both African literature and Afro-European literature cannot be understood outside the framework of consistent anti-imperialism.

10 *Post-colonial Politics & Culture*

Culture in Kenya, even during the colonial times, has always been an important theatre of political confrontation.

The infamous Berlin conference of 1884 saw the beginnings of formal British influence in Kenya, but the country was not really colonised until 1895. Of course it wasn't given to them. The British colonised Kenya by force. But right from the start, military and subsequently political domination went hand in hand with cultural repression. The route to effective control lay through cultural dominance. Wherever and whenever there were communal or national festivals, which of course meant a gathering of peoples, these were stopped. A good example was the Ituĩka ceremony in central Kenya which was banned by the British colonial authorities in 1925. The Ituĩka festival was held every thirty years or so to mark the handing over of power from one generation to another. This was enacted through songs, poetry and drama. So the ban meant the suppression of a whole cultural heritage that had taken generations to build. Under the colonial rule, then, native cultures were repressed while, through the school system, other imported traditions were encouraged. For instance, in the school that I went to, Scottish country dances were allowed even as the so-called tribal dances were banned.

One of the most important aspects of our pre-colonial literature was the oral tradition. Prior to the missionary presence in the country, there were very few languages, apart from Kiswahili, which had been reduced to writing. The oral tradition has always been very rich and it is not surprising that it was the one most utilised by the anti-colonial forces to make statements of resistance. Hence it was the oral tradition and the artists who operated within it that were the objects of colonial wrath. For instance in 1921, Harry Thuku, a leader of the workers' movement, was arrested and about 150 people killed at a march demanding his release. This confrontation was recorded in songs that in turn became very popular. One of the songs was called Kanyegenyūri. It was very beautiful, very well constructed, with very strong, colourful and erotic images describing the arrest of Harry Thuku and the demands for his release. It was mostly sung and danced by women and it became so powerful a statement of protest that it was banned by the colonial authorities. There was another called Mūthīrīgū. Again, a powerful combination of song, poetry and dance, mostly by young men. This became very popular particularly in central Kenya. It was also banned. Many people were actually arrested and put in prison for singing and dancing it. One of the verses defies threats of arrests and imprisonment:

> Even when we go to prison
> We shall still dance Mūthīrīgū

Both Kanyegenyūri and Mūthīrīgū are good examples of the culture of the oral tradition as a theatre of anti-colonial resistance, against colonial oppression.

Writers and books however were not spared. Between 1952 and 1962 political resistance took the form of armed struggle and this was led by the Mau Mau. This phase of the struggle had been preceded by a kind of cultural renaissance. Newspapers, for instance, and small publishing houses flourished. Books of poems and songs, in African languages, were brought out. It was a period of a literary upsurge. The energy came from the entire anti-colonial movement. Not surprisingly, when a state of emergency was declared in 1952, culture came under siege. Many books were banned. All the small presses publishing in African languages were closed down. All these books of poetry and songs were lost to Kenyans. Writers of the banned books were imprisoned without trial. The most prominent of them was Gakaara wa Wanjaū. He wrote in the Gīkūyū language during the colonial times and he continues to do so in the post-colonial period. As a writer, he has suffered both in the colonial era, detained without trial for nine years, and in post-colonial Kenya, imprisoned without trial for a month, badly tortured and then forced into a mysterious car accident. He survived it. He is therefore a very good example of political and cultural repression in Kenya, in both times, colonial and post-colonial. His fate symbolises the link between the two periods.

Post-colonial Kenya, economically and politically, saw in reality a continuation of colonial structures. Colonial society can be looked at as a social pyramid with the people divided on racial lines and occupying the different zones. The narrow part at the top was occupied by the white settler community, the middle part by the Asian community, and the broad base by the Africans. Now you can think of independence as simply the removal of the racial barriers to social mobility but the pyramid structure remaining the same. Some Africans could now climb up the pyramid to the middle and top zones. But there was hardly any mobility downwards. In other words the white community still occupies the room at the top, and the Asian community the middle zone. In short although there has been some movement upwards for some Africans and Asians, with some of them occupying positions of real economic and political power, the colonial social structure remained essentially the same. Now this has resulted in the political alienation of the majority at the base. The base remained dissatisfied. The very things that made the people take up arms against colonialism – external domination and internal repression – still exist.

This has been reflected in Kenyan culture, for instance in the kind of programmes encouraged by the post-colonial regimes. It is a culture that has reflected the dependence of the Kenyan economy and politics on outside influence. Western cultural dominance has been underwritten by the post-colonial political practices, for instance by what has been allowed on television, on film, and in educational programmes. What has happened in the area of language education and policy is a good example of this tendency. Before independence, African languages were taught for the first four years of the students' primary education. But after independence, African languages were abolished in schools. For years, until the policy was reversed, Kenyans were taught English from the nursery to university. One can imagine how hard it must have been for all those children. They were being programmed in the English language so that there was a complete break between the language they were actually using in their own homes, and the languages they were using in schools to conceptualise the world. Today there is a whole generation of Kenyan youth who live between two worlds. They may be perfect in the English language but the majority culture of post-colonial Kenya in which they live and work is not an English-speaking culture.

The result of this economic, political and cultural alienation of the majority from their post-colonial rulers has been a perfect replica of colonial practices. In order for the post-colonial regimes to maintain themselves in power they have had to repress democracy. They ensure that the people do not have much leeway in criticising, in organising, and even in simply expressing a different viewpoint. There can only be one viewpoint – that of the ruling regime. If they allow democratic practices, particularly in the electoral process, the people might express their dissatisfaction by returning to parliament a different party or leadership. Kenya is now a one-party state* with all the other political and social organisations banned or else integrated into the ruling party. It does not take too much imagination to see how this has affected culture. If it cannot allow people to express democracy in political life, the regime will certainly not allow democratic measures in the cultural life of the community. If there is a policy like the one we have in Kenya today where more than five people cannot meet without a police licence, then this automatically affects cultural practices as well. People cannot meet for a cultural activity, any cultural activity, without a licence. Whether they are meeting to write, to produce plays or to dance, the very fact of their having to have a licence in order to gather will adversely affect their creativity.

Thus, even what has happened in the culture of post-colonial Kenya is really a reproduction of colonial times. I will now cite a few examples. Songs were subversive in colonial times. Today songs have been found to be the most subversive element of Kenyan national life. In July 1990 for instance musicians were among those arrested and imprisoned simply because of their music. Many of the songs they sang were inspired by events in Muoroto, a small urban area of Nairobi, where a number of the dwellers were killed by the police. The government denied that there had been any killings. It even denied that there had been any fighting between the police and the people. Yet the people had seen it all. The musicians sang about the plight of the dwellers. Some of the songs had been couched in terms

*Since this talk was given, political parties have been allowed but still under repressive conditions.

of heaven and earth, devils and angels, the deadly combat between God and Satan. They were received and interpreted by the people in very earthly terms, certainly one not to the liking of the regime. In colonial times religious groups which had songs that carried a social message were objects of colonial repression. The same thing has been happening in post-colonial Kenya.

But it is in theatre that the struggle has most intensified. Indeed theatre and the place it has come to occupy in the political arena in post-colonial Kenya can only be compared with a similar position literature occupied in nineteenth-century Russia. Because of the repressive character of the Tsarist regime, literature became the cultural voice of the people. In between the hard covers of a literary text, characters could talk and argue about matters that no political party could talk about openly. This may explain why Russian literature came to be so highly valued in the country. In some ways theatre in post-colonial Kenya has come to occupy a similar position: with the banning of political parties and social organisations, theatre became the only arena outside the church and the mosque where two or more characters could argue out issues openly. People would go to the theatre expecting aesthetic packages of entertainment, but they would also find issues that were affecting their lives being debated. Not surprisingly the post-colonial regimes followed the footsteps of their colonial predecessors and came down heavily on the theatre.

In 1976, I was a member of a group that produced a play called *The Trial of Dedan Kīmathi*. We wanted to use the Kenya National Theatre, but at that time it was dominated by settler or allied settler interests with productions that included musicals such as *Annie Get Your Gun*, *The King and I*, *Alice in Wonderland*, and *Jesus Christ, Superstar*. We even had problems in securing space in the building. The struggle became so intense that it was taken up in newspaper articles. But even after the *The Trial of Dedan Kīmathi* was produced at the National Theatre, the director of the play, Seth Adagala, and I were called to CID headquarters and were specifically warned against interfering with European Theatre. In fact we had not interfered with European Theatre qua European Theatre. We were only guilty of offering Kenyan alternatives.

The difficulties with securing space at the National Theatre for Kenyan African plays, in part, made the Department of Literature at the University of Nairobi decide it would be better to take theatre to the people. Why quarrel over a building anyway? They developed what had already been tried at Makerere in Uganda long before – a travelling theatre. It was to be a free travelling theatre that would take plays to all parts of the country. This popularised theatre quite significantly. In 1977 some of us actually moved into the countryside. We worked at the University of Nairobi for a living but in theatre we worked at Kamīrīithū village where peasants and workers became involved in producing a play called *I Will Marry When I Want*. The play which reflected the contemporary social conditions of the working people as well as their history of resistance became very popular. I have written about this experience in several of my books, particularly in *Detained: A Writer's Prison Diary*, *Barrel of a Pen* and *Decolonising the Mind*. The play was banned and I myself was put in detention without trial between December 1977 and December 1978.

The repressive measures in the area of theatre became even more marked in 1982. After I came out of prison we tried to do another play called *Mother Sing For Me* by the same group of peasants and workers. We wanted to perform at the National Theatre. This time we were not even allowed to get onto the premises. We were locked out with the police waiting outside to see if we would force our way into the theatre or become involved in any rioting. So we moved to the University of Nairobi and continued to hold what we called public rehearsals which were of course open to everybody. There we were able to hold about ten performances before the police once again moved in and locked us out of the University of Nairobi. Thereafter the police went to Kamīrīithū village itself and razed the entire community theatre to the ground and banned any theatre events in the entire area. Our group was banned.

There are a few other examples all occurring in 1982. *Muntu* by Joe de Graft, which had been commissioned by All-Africa Conference of Churches in 1976 was now banned because it was allegedly talking about violence. A play written by some school children was banned and some of the students who had written the script suspended from the school. Al Amin Mazrui, the Kenyan linguist and playwright and a lecturer at Kenyatta University was imprisoned without trial three weeks after his own play, *Cry for Justice*, opened at the University of Nairobi. But of course since 1982 there have been more plays, particularly those in African languages, stopped by the regime.

Poets and other writers have not escaped the politics of culture in post-colonial Kenya. One of our leading poets. Abdulatif Abdulla, was imprisoned for three years in 1969 for writing and circulating a pamphlet called: *Kenya, Where Are We Heading To?* Asking questions is a dangerous exercise in a post-colonial society. You would think that all this would cripple Kenyan Literature?

In a strange kind of way these repressive conditions have seen a rebirth of a kind of national literature in the country. For instance the theatre which has developed under these conditions has been very progressive in form and content. Jails have produced a whole tradition of prison literature. When Abdulatif Abdulla was imprisoned, he wrote poems later published as a book under the title *Voice of Agony*, and which, ironically, later won the Jomo Kenyatta prize for literature. When I was imprisoned I wrote the novel *Devil on the Cross*. Some of you may know that it was then that I decided not to write any more plays or creative works in the English language; that I would in future write in Gĩkũyũ and other African languages. This decision and the debate arising from it have revived the tradition of writing in African languages in Kenya, although it is still not the dominant trend. In 1986 following another wave of intensified repression, many more academics were imprisoned. Some of them, on coming out, are writing their memoirs.

There are many other writers who have been forced into exile and no doubt this will produce its own kind of literature. For those who remain, there is the question of self-censorship. They have to be very careful about what they say and how they say it. The extreme form of self-censorship is silence. There is of course the category of writers who have chosen to work with the repressive regime. In fact one of our leading writers in Kenya is a Minister of Culture.

And so in post-colonial Kenya one cannot really speak of uniformity of writers, because they don't actually occupy the same position *vis-à-vis* cultural repression. They have taken very contradictory and often conflicting positions. One can only meaningfully say there are two types of writers in Kenya today. There are the official writers, or officially approved writers; and the unofficial ones, that is those who are not accepted by the government.

All this demonstrates the complexity of the politics of culture in a post-colonial society. The situation cannot be properly understood outside the framework of the neo-colonial economic and political structures which are, in effect, colonial structures under another name.

11 In Moi's Kenya, History is Subversive

Why is history subversive?

Human beings make history by their actions on nature and on themselves. History is therefore about human struggle: first with nature as the material source of the wealth they create, food, clothing and shelter; and secondly, struggle with other humans over the control of that wealth. Labour, human labour, is the key link between the two struggles. It is labour, with all the instruments and accumulated skills, that makes wealth out of nature. The struggle among humans is over control of the entire organisation of the production, exchange and distribution of the fruits of labour.

Development in society is brought about by changes in the human struggle with nature; and in the social struggle. The changing social formations, institutions, values, outlook, reflect the ever-changing relationships between labour and nature, and between social groups in one nation and between nations.

Change, movement, is hence the eternal theme in history. It is the universal expressed in all the particularities of the various nations and people of the earth over the centuries. Therefore no society is ever static: there is movement all the time since the two relations or struggles are ever active. History is ever reminding The Present of any society: even you shall come to pass away. Tomorrow will be The Present; and The Present will be The Yesterday.

But it is precisely because history is the result of struggle and tells of change that it is perceived as a threat by all the ruling strata in all the oppressive exploitative systems. Tyrants and their tyrannical systems are terrified at the sound of the wheels of history. History is subversive. And it is because it is actually subversive of the existing tyrannical system that there have been attempts to arrest it. But how can one arrest the wheels of history? So they try to *rewrite* history, make up *official* history; if they can put cottonwool in their ears and in those of the population, maybe *they* and *the people* will not hear the *real* call of history, will not hear the *real* lessons of history.

Kenya, under British colonialism and now under neo-colonialism, is a good example.

If there is one consistent theme in the history of Kenya over the last four hundred years or so (since the sixteenth century), it is surely one of the Kenyan peoples' struggle against foreign domination. At various times and places, they have fought against the Arab, Portuguese and British invaders. The British invasion in the nineteenth century and their colonial occupation in the first half of the twentieth century were accompanied by the heroic resistance of Kenyan people of all nationalities. Some names, like those of Waiyaki, Koitalel, Hassan, Me Katilili have become legends. Brilliant battles were fought. Fortifications built by Bukusu nationality around Mount Elgon, for instance, still stand as a reminder of Kenya's heroic tradition of resistance and struggle.

And during the years of British settler occupation, the resistance was continued, acquiring a new character because a new class, a wage-earning class (a proletariat) was born with colonial capitalism. The new working class joined hands with peasants and tried to forge links with the workers and peasants of all the nationalities to overcome the divide-and-rule tactics of British colonialism. The highest peak of this heroic tradition of resistance was the armed struggle initiated and carried out by the Kenya Land Freedom Army (KLFA), otherwise widely known as Mau Mau. The supreme leader of Kenya Land Freedom Army was Dedan Kĩmathi.

But of course there has been another tradition: *Sell-Out*, a traitorous tradition whose highest expression was in the actions of the homeguard, loyalist collaborators with the British enemy, which are continued in the neo-colonial system suffocating millions of Kenyans today.

British colonialism tried to cover up the true history of Kenya. They tried to rewrite Kenya's history to justify their invasion and subsequent occupation of the country. *Kenya Land Freedom Army*, the first of its kind in the post-Second World War period in Africa,

97

became the focus of British propaganda, to prevent armed struggle becoming a model for a form of resistance. The British even trained some Kenyans and brought them up to look at Kenya history with the eyes of the British bourgeoisie. The British propaganda history consisted of burying the real tradition of struggle and, erecting in its place, the tradition of loyalist collaboration. Loyalist historians were praised, honoured, while the people's historians were incarcerated.

This attempt to bury the living soul of Kenya's history of struggle and resistance, and the attempt to normalise the tradition of loyalism to imperialism has continued into neo-colonial Kenya. The loyalist colonial homeguards of yesterday are the neo-colonial Mbwa Kalis (guard dogs) of imperialism today. There have been two types of history in Kenya: the *real living* history of the masses; and the *approved official* history. Those who run neo-colonialism are mortally afraid of any symbols or reminders of the Kenya peoples' history of struggle and resistance. And naturally, KLFA (Mau Mau) and Dedan Kĩmathi, as the highest symbols of that tradition, have received total official neglect or distortion.

The two types of histories have produced two types of historians. There are the official historians, the approved state historians, whose role is to give rational legitimacy to the tradition of loyalism and collaboration with imperialism. These have received state accolades and honours.

But the Kenya people's real history of struggle and resistance has thrown up its own historians. First are the ordinary people who, in their songs, poems, stories, sayings, anecdotes, remembrances, still talk of the Waiyakis; the Koitalels; the Me Katililis; the Hassans and the Kĩmathis of Kenya history. And secondly, a few progressive intellectuals who have negated their roots among the petty-bourgeoisie, and joined hands with the people. These have put their learning, their intellect, at the service of the people. They are committed to unearthing the buried history of struggle and resistance.

In Guyana we have the example of Walter Rodney. In Kenya we have the example of Maina wa Kĩnyattĩ. Since his return to Kenya in the 1970s, Maina wa Kĩnyattĩ saw his role as that of being the ears and eyes of the people as far as this concerned their history. Whereas the official state historians borrowed eyes and ears from the colonial and neo-colonial heritage, Maina wa Kĩnyattĩ and other patriotic historians, borrowed their eyes and ears from the people. Maina wa Kĩnyattĩ travelled extensively in Kenya. He spent many an evening and week-ends in the homes of those who had fought the British and who were now condemned to living in hovels, and on the edges of starvation. He recorded their stories. They in turn came to trust him. They started giving him documents they had hidden for years. They gave him information they had kept among themselves for fear of official, neo-colonial wrath. They knew that those holding the reins of power in post-independent Kenya were those actually sabotaging the struggle for independence. But here was a historian who seemed not afraid; who was talking their language of struggle.

The papers Maina wa Kĩnyattĩ was able to rescue are contained in his book. They speak for themselves. They need no introduction, or defence or explanation. It is a record of how the participants, the Kenya Land Freedom Army, saw the struggle as contained in some of their written documents.

Theirs was a national struggle: for land, independence, freedom from hunger, freedom from foreign control, freedom from external and internal social oppression, and they put their lives at the service of those ideals of political liberation.

They were completely surrounded by the enemy. Unlike the armed liberation movements that followed them in Africa (in Algeria, Mozambique, Angola, Guinea-Bissau, Zimbabwe, etc) they had no rear or supply bases in neighbouring countries, for the simple reason that these were also under the same colonial enemy. Their bases were entirely among the Kenyan people.

For arms they depended almost totally on what they could capture from the British army, and on their own factories in the liberated and semi-liberated zones around Mount Kenya and Kirinyaga.

Again, they had hardly any easy access to national and international propaganda to counter the stream of lies coming from the British settler colonial regime in Kenya and the Colonial Office in London. In the country, KLFA depended mostly on word of mouth to explain their case and the progress of the struggle to Kenyan people. But still, with all the limitations under which they operated, they tried to keep written records of these activities; and to establish written communications with the national and the international community.

Some of the documents were later captured by the colonial enemy. Some were destroyed, or distorted. Some are still held in secret by the British government and the neo-colonial regime in Kenya. But some escaped capture; and it is to the credit of Maina wa Kĩnyattĩ that he managed to recover a number of these letters and documents and put them at the disposal of the Kenyan and the international community.

When the history of the armed liberation struggles in Africa is finally written, KLFA will stand supreme, not so much because of the heights it reached but because of the depths from which it rescued Kenya and Africa. KLFA (Mau Mau) was the first organised armed blow against imperialism in Africa. In this they showed the way which was later followed with such brilliant results in Algeria, Mozambique, Angola, Guinea-Bissau, Zimbabwe, and in South Africa today.

Maina wa Kĩnyattĩ* has now paid a price for his work in Kenya history. In 1982, he was arrested, and imprisoned for six years. He just about escaped the fate of another historian of the people, Walter Rodney from Guyana. But has he? He is losing his eyesight. His health has been deteriorating. Conditions in Kenya prisons are among the worst in the world.

Those who have imprisoned him hope that he will lose sight of the Real History of Kenya. But they are wrong. These documents and his other works like *Thunder from the Mountains; Mau Mau Patriotic Songs* and *Mau Mau: The Highest Peak of Resistance*, will always stand as a memorial of his commitment and courage.

But even if they were to silence Maina wa Kĩnyattĩ, would they silence the history of Kenya? Would they arrest, imprison the living history of Kenya? This history is being written by the millions of workers and peasants of all the nationalities in Kenya who in their actions and songs are saying 'No' to imperialism and its comprador alliances in Kenya. The spirit of the Kenya Land Freedom Army (KLFA) and its leader Dedan Kĩmathi is being reborn in Kenya today!!

History *is* subversive because *truth* is! The unavenged father's ghost of Kimathi's struggle and his KLFA, walks the days and nights of today's neo-colonial Kenya. The masses know it. So, too, do the

*He was released in October 1989.

ruling comprador bourgeoisie. Hence the continuing repression; and its opposite – *resistance*. The 1990s will see the conflict played out to its logical conclusion – liberation from neo-colonialism. Maina wa Kīnyattī's papers will play their part in that struggle by providing lessons from the weaknesses and strengths; the failures and the successes of the past.

12 *From the Corridors of Silence*

The Exile Writes Back

I had come to Britain to promote the English translation of my novel, *Devil On The Cross*, originally written in Gĩkũyũ at Kamĩtĩ Maximum Security prison in Kenya in 1978. Heinemann, my publishers, had put me up at the Russell Hotel so that I could be near their offices at Bedford Square and to the press. But the book that first caught my eye on entering a London bookshop was a slim volume titled *Writers In Exile*, by Andrew Gurr. I was surprised, on leafing through it, to find myself in the company of Katherine Mansfield from New Zealand and V.S. Naipaul from Trinidad, as those modern writers who had followed the path set by the Irish writer, James Joyce: that of flight to the metropolis of a foreign country. You remember the position of Joyce's hero in *A Portrait of the Artist As a Young Man*?

> I will tell you what I will do and what I will not do. I will not serve that in which I no longer believe, whether it call itself my home, my fatherland or my church; and I will try to express myself in some mode of life or art as freely as I can and as wholly as I can, using for my defence the only arms I allow myself to use – silence, exile and cunning.

Home, father/motherland, exile? I, a writer in exile? I had just arrived in Britain on June 8, firmly intending to leave for Kenya on 31 July. In my book, *Detained: A Writer's Prison Diary*, published the same year as Andrew Gurr's *Writers In Exile*, I had rejected the option of exile into which the Kenya government has been trying to force me by denying me jobs, virtually banning me from the premises of schools and colleges. I was even feeling not a little pleased with myself for having confirmed the date and the flight of my return home. I was not going to be one of James Joyce's heroes, obeying only the laws of my imagination on the banks of the Thames or Seine, or in a new Bloomsbury around Bedford Square.

I took time off from the busy schedule of interviews and talks to visit the late C.L.R. James at his place in Railton Road, Brixton. I had first met him in Makerere University in 1969 where I then held a one-year fellowship in creative writing. He was on a brief visit.

We readily found common ground in our interest in Caribbean literature and Pan-Africanist politics. And now, in 1982, James readily recalled our conversations in Makerere, particularly about his old comrade-in-Pan-Africanism, the late Jomo Kenyatta, about whom James did not always have the most endearing of things to say.

I had fallen out with the Kenyatta regime in 1969 over the suppression of academic freedom at the University of Nairobi and I had resigned in protest. In 1977 Kenyatta had imprisoned me for my activities in community theatre at Limuru, in Kenya, although some other people argue that it was my novel, *Petals of Blood*, which had really angered the regime.

I briefed James about the intensified repression under the new Moi regime. I told him about the recent wave of arrests which had led to the detention without trial of a number of intellectuals, including Al Amin Mazrui, a Kenyan playwright. 'And you are still intending to go back on July 31?' he asked, slightly raising his frail body from the bed. 'They will kill you in six months, the way they did Walter Rodney.' I would go home, I insisted. On parting he gave me one of his books with the inscription: 'For Ngugi. Please stay for a while at least. Today we need you here.' The book was a critical evaluation of Melville's *Moby Dick*, a novel we used to read as an exam text in Kenya in the fifties.

On arrival in my hotel, I found an urgent coded message from Kenya: 'A red carpet awaits you at Jomo Kenyatta airport on your return.' Later I was able to confirm the message: I was due for arrest and another detention without trial, or worse . . . It took a while for the reality of the message to sink in. I could not accept the fact of exile, or the pleasures of exile as George Lamming once described it in a book. And even after I had cancelled my return and progressively descended from my residency in the Russell Hotel to a wanderer in London in search of a place in which to live, I could not bring myself to use the word 'exile' in reference to myself.

'Shipwrecked' was the word I often used, perhaps remembering James's mariners, renegades, and castaways. But the fact is that I was now living the reality of the modern writer in Africa.

Such a writer was born in captivity in more ways than one. The twentieth-century African literature, particularly that in European languages, has roots in nineteenth-century slave narratives by the likes of Olaudah Equiano. In his autobiography, *The Interesting Life of Olaudah Equiano, or Gustavus Vassa, the African*, he wrote of the Africa of his childhood as consisting of nations of dancers, musicians and poets, very much in terms that would later become the central themes of the Negritude writers of the thirties and forties. But while Equiano's prison-house was the entire landscape *outside* Africa, for many writers their prison-house is inside their countries.

The twentieth century has seen many an African writer confined by the colonial and neo-colonial state to corridors of silence. Thus British Kenya saw many of the militant Mau Mau in jails and detention camps in the fifties; apartheid South Africa has at various times jailed writers like Dennis Brutus, Caesarina Kona Makhoere, and the late Alex La Guma; independent Kenya imprisoned writers like Abdulatif Abdulla and Al Amin Mazrui; Egypt ensured a taste of prison for such writers as Sherif Hetata and Nawal el Saadawi; Kofi Awoonor from Ghana has also had a prison experience; and currently Jack Mapanje of Malawi is languishing in prison*. And there have been classic cases of writers like Gakaara wa Wanjaũ of Kenya, who were jailed by both the colonial and neo-colonial authorities for their writing.

These are only a few representative examples from East, West, South, and North Africa. These prison graduates have produced a literature born of their experiences in the corridors of silence. It is telling that the first African recipient of the Nobel Prize for Literature, Wole Soyinka, is himself a prison graduate, having spent three years in various jails in Nigeria, the land from which Equiano had been abducted in the eighteenth century. Thus, just as there is a

---

*Jack Mapanje was released in May 1991.

tradition of slave narratives, there is in the twentieth century a whole tradition of prison literature from Africa.

Unfortunately a few other writers never survived their prison-houses to tell the tale. Idi Amin's Uganda had a number of writers killed, just as in South Africa today. Which of the two would have been my fate – prison or death – had I returned to Moi's Kenya, I am not too keen to know.

I had spent a year in a maximum security prison in 1977–78 and I know how much of a waste of human life prison is, especially in Kenya where the jailing of intellectuals has been a punitive measure. Perhaps James was right but I didn't want to try to prove him wrong.

What finally convinced me about the truth of the messages of a red-carpet welcome in 1982 by President Moi at Jomo Kenyatta airport was the flight into exile of two writers, Kĩmani Gecau and Ngũgĩ wa Mĩriĩ. I had worked with both at the community theatre in Limuru in Kenya. They had been only one or two steps ahead of Moi's agents. Kĩmani and Ngũgĩ had become part of the community of African writers in exile.

I am here talking about physical exile. There have been two types of writers in exile from Africa. There are the voluntary exiles, those forced to live abroad through choice or through circumstances other than threats of prison or death. These are the ones who are comparable to the expatriate writer of the James Joyce or Hemingway tradition, or that of the Bloomsbury circle of Katherine Mansfield.

In the twenties and thirties, the group of African students who lived in Paris produced a literature that later acquired the semblance of a distinctive movement under the name Negritude. Sédar Senghor, later the president of Senegal, was one of the leading lights of this expatriate type of literature.

The second category is that of those writers forced into exile through fear of certain death or prison or both. These are victims of state terror and they are in flight for their lives. They belong to the category of Brecht and others who fled Nazi Germany. From them there has not been any distinctive literary movement, I suppose because they do not always come from similar circumstances.

Nevertheless physical exile has been part and parcel of twentieth-century African literature. Beginning with Peter

Abrahams, South Africa has contributed most to this category. *Home and Exile* is the title of a book by another South African writer, Lewis Nkosi, and it very well captures the underlying themes and contradictions in modern African literature.

Home? Even after I had accepted that I had been shipwrecked on an island called Great Britain, I could never bring myself to unpack the bags I had kept ready for my return to Kenya.

Then in 1983/84 I wrote *Matigari*, a novel of return, in the Gĩkũyũ language, and I felt a sense of belonging such as I had felt when in 1978 at Kamĩtĩ Maximum Security Prison in Cell No. 16, I had written *Caitaani Mũtharabainĩ* (*Devil on the Cross*) as an attempt to reconnect myself to the community from which I had been so brutally cut by the neo-colonial regime in Kenya. Now I had done the same thing and experienced not too dissimilar emotions. Was there a connection between *prison* and *exile*?

In both cases the writer is keenly aware of his loss of freedom. He is haunted by a tremendous longing for a connection. Exile can even be worse than prison. Some people have been known to survive prison in their own countries better than 'freedom' in physical exile.

But there is another sense, a larger sense, in which we can talk of exile in African literature. The writers who emerged after the Second World War were nearly all the products of universities at home and abroad. Some of these universities like Ibadan in Nigeria, Makerere in Uganda, Achimota in Ghana had been set up to manufacture an elite that could later make a good partnership with the British ruling circles. The curricula reflected little or nothing of the local surroundings.

The situation was quite ironic. Many of the educated Africans had been sent to the higher seats of learning by their peasant communities so they could come back and help in the collective survival. But at the end of the educational pipe-line, these select few had more in common with the very social forces which had kept their communities down in the first place. In colonial times they would probably have joined the state administration as junior partners, but with the hope that a little bit more would fall to them from the master's table. In neo-colonial times – that is, after independence – they joined the multinationals whose profits depended on the misery of the very people who had sent them out to bring back their share.

Writers were part of the educated elite, and there was no way they could escape from these contradictions. For instance, they nearly all opted for European languages as the means of their creative output. Thus English, French, and Portuguese became the languages of the new African literature. But these languages were spoken by only about 5 per cent of the population. The African Prometheus had been sent to wrest fire from the gods, but instead became a captive contented with warming himself at the fireside of the gods. Otherwise he carried the fire in containers that were completely sealed and for which the majority had no key. For whom were they writing?

I was a student at Leeds University in the mid-sixties when I first strongly felt a sense of despair at that contradiction in my situation as a writer. I had just published *A Grain of Wheat*, a novel that dealt with the Kenya people's struggle for independence. But the very people about whom I was writing were never going to read the novel or have it read for them. I had carefully sealed their lives in a linguistic case. Thus whether I was based in Kenya or outside, my opting for English had already marked me as a writer in exile. Perhaps Andrew Gurr had been right after all. The African writer is already set aside from people by his education and language choice.

The situation of the writer in twentieth-century Africa mirrors that of the larger society. For if the writer has been in a state of exile – whether it is physical or spiritual – the people themselves have been in exile in relationship to their economic and, political landscape.

During the colonial era, the African people were dispossessed of their land and labour and mind. The colonial power took on the form of an inaccessible god, set on dismembering a people and a continent. The remnant of this Africa can still be seen in South Africa.

But independence did not always result in the empowerment of the people. Economic power still lay in the hands of multinationals, and political power in the hands of a tiny elite exercising it on behalf of the dominant interests of the West. This elite, pampered with military gadgets of all kinds with which to reign in a restive population, has often turned an entire country into a vast prison-house. Africa is a continent alienated from itself by years of alien conquests and internal despots. Thus the state of exile in the literary landscape reflects a larger state of alienation in the society as a whole, a clear case of colonial legacy which has left scars on the body, heart, and mind of the continent. *The Man Died*; *Things Fall Apart*; *No Longer at Ease*; *The Beautyful Ones Are Not Yet Born*; *From a Crooked Rib*; the titles of many novels in Africa speak clearly of this alienation, or this dismemberment of parts that could have made a whole.

Is African literature capable of a successful homecoming? It has already gone through at least three phases within the last three or four decades. In the fifties its sentiments – Tell Freedom – were largely in harmony with the general sentiments for independence. The sixties, the era of *coups d'état*, gave birth to a literature of disillusionment. Attacks and lamentation were the key tones in this literature. The seventies and the eighties saw some writers seeking to find a way out of the earlier despair by trying to connect the works of the imagination with the struggles of the people for social change and social justice. But their search for a way back among the people was hampered by the very linguistic prison they had been thrown into by their colonial legacy.

The nineties will see more and more writers trying to break out of the linguistic prison to seek their genuine roots in the languages and rhythms of life of the dispossessed majority. Only in this way will African literature find its real homecoming among the African masses who have always struggled to overcome the state of alienation. Otherwise it is doomed to die, or stagnate in the linguistic prison of its colonial legacy.

The nightmare of the latter half of the twentieth century is the fear that a human creation, the Bomb, has come to threaten the very existence of the human race, and indeed all life. A universal sense of exile, of not really belonging, still haunts humankind.

In its search for a genuine homecoming, African literature will truly reflect the universal struggle for a world which truly belongs to us all.

13 *Imperialism & Revolution*

Movements for Social Change

In 1986, three young men were hauled into court in Kenya charged with engaging in acts of sabotage against the ruling neo-colonial regime. The three, Tirop arap Kitur, Samuel Mūngai and Karīmi Nduthu, remained splendidly defiant, and, to borrow words from an account of a similar situation, 'as the trial went on, the roles were reversed: those who came to accuse found themselves accused, and the accused became the accusers!' Karīmi Nduthu told the kangaroo court 'I love Kenya. Truth must be told without fear. *Change like death is inevitable.*'

Those words were very much in my mind in accepting the invitation to open the Sixth International Book Fair of Radical, Black and Third World Books whose theme is 'Movement for Social Change'. Change, it has been observed, is the constant theme in nature, society and human thought. Everything changes.

Our own century, the twentieth century, has been one of such great and spectacular changes as were only the stuff of dreams, myths, and fantasies in earlier centuries. Science and technology have wrought great changes in our relationship to nature and the universe. National struggles have brought about changes in the relationship between countries. And social struggles have brought about even greater changes in relationships between different classes in the same country.

In terms of social change, the present face of the twentieth century is a product of the struggle between two contending forces. On the one hand, imperialism which saw the elevation not simply of the non-producer but of the parasitic non-producer into the dominant ruling power not just over people from one country but over several nations, races and countries. On the other has been social revolution which for the first time in human history sought change and often fought for power on behalf and from the standpoint of the producer working peoples.

Let us look at the two phenomena: Imperialism and Revolution. Capitalism entered its imperialist stage towards the end of the nineteenth century. The Berlin Conference and the division of Africa into spheres of European influence and the subsequent colonisation was its external political expression. The reign of finance capital with its home base in Europe and abroad had begun.

Imperialism is the power of dead capital. A few shareholders in the City and Wall Street by merely manipulating and playing the monopoly game of sale and purchase of stocks and shares can determine the location, death and life of industries; they can determine who eats, what and where. They can create famines, deserts, pollution, and wars. The peasant in the remotest part of the globe is affected by the power of those who hoard billions even though only visible in figures on computer screens in the finance houses we call banks. Currently, the IMF, the World Bank, are determining the lives and deaths of many in Africa, Asia and South America.

Imperialism has maintained its power in three ways:

It feeds on colonies and neo-colonies. In colonies yesterday and neo-colonies today, imperialism through its ruling agents in Asia, Africa and South America supports any and every anti-people barbarity. Thousands can be massacred in say Kenya and imperialism will continue propping such anti-people regimes in the name of stability. The South African apartheid regime could not last a day without the support of imperialist nations.

It also arms itself to the teeth to protect its power against rival imperialism or from real or imagined threats from successful people-based revolutions. The arms race is a race against human life. Those who for instance have insisted on nuclear weapons are saying: 'better to profit by human death than profit human life'.

And third, in its own home (say in the USA, Western Europe and Japan), imperialism protects its power from threats of people's power by social oppression, racism, sexism, and even through religious divisions. Police violence against the population and sections of the population is a fact of life in all the heartlands of imperialism. Racism and even gender discrimination like women's oppression is

110

not an accident but a product of imperialism in its home base. These social oppressions are exported to neo-colonies where in South American military republics or in South Africa, they can be seen in all their naked glory.

But pitted against imperialism have been forces for meaningful social change. Dead capital, moribund capitalism, has been challenged and often successfully so, by living labour. Through the various movements for social change in the world, life has been triumphing over death. Working people's power is the revolutionary alternative and challenge to moneyocracy of imperialism.

In the twentieth century, there have been three broad but inter-related movements for social change:

First have been movements which have sought and brought about successful social revolutions – that is social transformation. The greatest, because it ushered a new era in the twentieth century, was the 1917 Russian Revolution. But it was followed by others: China and Cuba for instance. Thus the gory dawn of imperialism at the beginning of the twentieth century with its near total control of the world through colonies, semi-colonies and other dependencies, saw the rosy dawn of its opposite: revolutionary people's power.

Second, there have been national liberation movements in two stages – movements for independence from *colonialism* and those for national democratic revolutions against *neo-colonialism*. Many of the Third World movements fall within this category. South Africa is a unique case which sees a convergence of all the above features: a people's movement against colonialism, neo-colonialism and for revolutionary change. And that is why South African people's struggles are really the story of our lives: a metaphor of the twentieth century.

And, third, within the belly of the beast, that is within the imperialist nations and countries, there have been democratic forces for change. The social democratic gains in Western Europe after the Second World War was a response to these democratic forces. Today, working class struggles; women's movements; Black people's movements; the peace movement, are all part of the democratic forces for change.

All the three major movements – revolutionary, national liberation, and democratic – are different stages of the same struggle of the living labour of the majority against the dead capital of a parasitic few.

In all the three movements, Black and Third World peoples have been at the centre. For instance, all the successful major social revolutions in the twentieth century, apart from the Russian Revolution, have been in the Third World: China, North Korea, Vietnam, Cuba are well known examples. The independence struggles in Africa, Asia and South America against old colonialism have already changed the political map of the twentieth century while the current struggles for national democratic revolutions against neo-colonialism will vastly change the power equation in the world. Everywhere people's power is knocking at the door as we move towards the twenty-first century.

And lastly, in the imperialist countries – like USA and Western Europe – Black people's movements and others involving people of Third World origins are challenging the racist anti-people structures and in the process bringing about rumblings of profound changes to come. The civil rights movement of the sixties in the USA did affect and continues to affect the general politics of the country. Even within the limited democracy of presidential elections in the USA, it was a black presidential candidate, Jesse Jackson, who, through the concept of a Rainbow Coalition, was to articulate the centrality of people of African, Asian and South American origins, in the struggle for people's power in the USA. 'Our Time Has Come' was an apt rallying call. Here in Britain, the rise of black people's organisations in the seventies and eighties is already affecting the vocabulary and the terms by which the struggle for people's power is being perceived and fought for. Black is coming back, somebody wrote of the black democratic upsurge in the USA of the sixties and the same, at a higher level, can be said of black people's assertions, struggles and challenges for real changes in this society.

All the three major movements outlined above have been accompanied by an explosion of artistic talents and general intellectual creativity. The emergence of African writers in African and European languages after the Second World War cannot be divorced from the great anti-imperialist movements for independence. The revolutions in Cuba, China and Vietnam gave rise to new talents and creativity in all the different areas of the arts. The social struggles in the USA and those in Britain have been accompanied by similar explosions of talents and artistic movements, and our presence here today is a testimony to this.

112

What is important has been the convergence of the Black and Third World peoples' political and artistic movements within Western countries and those from inside Africa and the Third World countries themselves.

It has been clearer in politics for instance with the Pan-Africanism in the heyday of the anti-colonial struggles. But parallel to the Pan-African political movements were also artistic movements. The Black Writers Congresses in Rome and Paris in 1956 and 1959; the FESTAC in Dakar and Lagos in 1966 and 1976; were all manifestations of that independent search for an anti-imperialist unifying artistic sensibility. The strengthening of the *links that bind us* in the area of politics and the arts can only strengthen the movement for social change.

The International Book Fair of Radical, Black and Third World Books is a continuation of that convergence and a further strengthening of the links that bind us.

But in some ways the Book Fair is more unique because it has given and it continues to give that convergence of radical political and artistic sensibility from Africa, Asia, South America and Europe, an institutional form so that it is an annual event, and a concrete form by way of a meeting of real books, real writers and thinkers in flesh and blood, from the four continents. At the same time the Fair, as you can see, is people-based and it is organised by real movements that are actually engaged in daily struggles here in Britain. The Fair itself is an example of a twentieth-century movement for social change as well as being a reflection and a product of social struggles and changes in Asia, South America and Europe.

III

Freeing Culture from Racism

14 *The Ideology of Racism*

War on Peace Within & Among Nations

There once lived a short-sighted colonial farmer who on Sunday mornings would stand on the prostrate bodies of his gardeners to look through the window and enjoy the sight of the vast tea plantation that spread out from the manorial house. 'What a beautiful day, so peaceful', he would murmur genuinely moved by the apparent stability all round. So absorbed was he by the peace that he could not hear the rumblings of their tummies or their silent groans of discontent. 'A peaceful country, don't you think', he would say turning to the house servants who stood by ready to serve him his breakfast. And the house servants would also stand on some of the bodies but at a respectful distance from the master and they would chorus back: 'Yes master, peace'.

Today that colonial farmer could be one of the white masters of apartheid standing on the backs of millions of blacks in South Africa and Namibia, shouting peace while carrying out war against the people. Or he could be the West standing on the backs of Asia, Africa and South America shouting peace while arming their favourite puppets who carry out war against the people. Or he could be the Euroamerican or any national ruling class standing on the backs of the vast working majority shouting peace while arming themselves to the teeth to protect the status quo of the few over the many within the nation and among nations.

These talk of peace today. But where is the peace for the millions of victims of apartheid? Where is the peace for the black people in Britain, Continental Europe, North America? Where is the peace for the millions and millions under the cruel neo-colonial regimes in Asia, Africa and South America? Where is the peace for millions

116

in the most advanced industrial nations who are jobless and home-less? Where is the peace for the working people who make the wealth of nations and yet shiver and starve?

The fact is that all these people live in a permanent state of war waged against them through two kinds of fatal weapons: the instruments of mental and spiritual subjugation and the instruments of physical suppression.

First take the weapon of mental and spiritual subjugation. This is the ideological weapon and it comes wrapped up in many forms: as religion, the arts, the media, culture, values, beliefs, even as feelings. Racism is one of the most devastating of all the ideological weapons wielded by imperialism today and it is meant to safeguard the entire system of exploitation of the many by the few in one nation and among nations. Racism is a conscious ideology of imperialism with five interlinked features.

One is obscurantism. Racism obscures the real relationship between the wealth of the few and the poverty of the many within a capitalist nation; and, internationally, between the wealth of Western nations and the poverty of the majority of nations in Asia, Africa and South America.

Within a single nation, say a Western nation, racism is part of the entire strategem that obscures the obvious fact (except, of course, when there are strikes and whole industries come to a halt) that the labour of the majority produces and the capital of the few disposes. But through all sorts of mental manipulations, reality is turned upside down, making it seem as if it is the capital of the few that produces the wealth of that nation and not the labour of the majority. Workers are therefore expected to be grateful to the owners of capital for creating jobs and hence wages. Where there is a black segment (or any easily recognisable foreign, racial, religious segment among the workers) it is expected to exhibit even servility and gratitude because, by and large, the capital engaging that labour is white-controlled. Propagandists of capital talk and write as if black labour ought to kneel down in eternal gratitude to the white god of capital. White workers might even come to identify with the whiteness of capital against the blackness of labour. In time this is shortened to an easy racist formula: blacks ought to be grateful to whites. The fact that black labour produces is obscured by the racist formula.

Between the Western capitalist nations and the Third World countries, racism obscures the fact that the wealth of Europe and America (and Japan) is partly made out of the labour of Asia, Africa and South America. The wealth of the West is rooted in the poverty of the rest of us. This is true historically. Western Europe and North America accumulated capital through the slave trade, slave labour and colonial labour. It is still true today through the neo-colonial arrangements that still bind Africa to the West in a partnership of the rider and the horse. But here again, as in a racially divided nation, reality is turned upside down. Propagandists of Western capital make it seem as if it is their capital which creates wealth in the 'Third' World. Such countries, bled daily into ever-mounting poverty, are nevertheless expected to show gratitude to that Western capital, meaning the West, and since by and large the West is European, the expected abject relations are reduced to the same racist formula but now in the international context: Asia and Africa ought be grateful to Europe. Asian and African labour needs white capital but never the other way round. The false formula once accepted, the neo-colonial ruling elites in the 'Third' World will do almost anything, murder their own people even, to create stability for Western capital. Black gratitude to white charity becomes a national ideal and the expected basis of international relations between the West and the rest of us, to borrow the phrase from Chinweizu's book of the same title. Neo-colonialism adds considerable stains of blood to those that Western capital already acquired through the slave trade, slavery and colonialism.

Obscurantism leads us to the other feature of racism: divide and rule. Racism obscures not only the real relationship between capital and labour, but also the relations that bind capital to capital and more importantly the links of labour to labour under the sway of the same financial and industrial conglomerates, nationally and internationally. The aim is to make labour see itself in national, racial, religious, or tribal enclaves.

Within a nation, workers of a given racial or religious section are put into a more priveleged position, for instance being assured of job security, better pay, promotional opportunities, easier access to housing, *vis-à-vis* others of a different skin pigmentation, or mode of speech or accent. These priveleges, or advantages, are not of course paid for from profits but from lowering the wages of another section of the workers. Definite attitudes begin to grow on the foundation of that differentiation or discrimination and these may develop into a system of assumptions about the racial character of the other. Mutual suspicions among the workers begin and these are passed on and may become a tradition. Workers begin to defend their job security against other workers. Workers begin to resent demands from other workers for solidarity, for such a solidarity might jeopardise their own seemingly secure jobs, and this is particularly so in times of hardship. This division between workers of different racial groups has been raised to the status of philosophy and political practice in apartheid South Africa. The result of this bribe and take is the divide and rule tactics employed against the workers within the same nation.

But the same tactics of bribe and take, divide and rule, can also be seen at work at the international level. Essentially the working people of the colonies, semi-colonies and neo-colonies and the working people of Europe and North America often face the same capital with identical ownership. For instance, the financial institutions in New York, London, Paris, Bonn, Tokyo, are largely the same as those in Lagos, Nairobi, Johannesburg, Cairo, Manila, Seoul. The same is true for industrial and commercial enterprises. Thus, in most cases, the worker in Kenya, South Africa, South Korea, the Philippines, Chile, Brazil, El Salvador, and the worker in Western Europe or North America and Japan are engaged by the same institutions, really the same employer or group of employers. But racism, while obscuring the links that bind working people, adds to the divisions by ensuring differentiation in the rewards given to global labour on racial lines. The great divide between the West and the 'Third' World or between North and South, depending on one's favourite euphemism, wears a racial camouflage: it is largely the whites of European stock versus the dark races of the earth. The huge profits extracted from the workers in Asia, Africa and South America are brought back to Europe and North America and Japan and help in raising the standard of living of the West as a whole. The working class in Europe, North America and Japan becomes the international labour aristocracy *vis-à-vis* the workers of the colonies, semi-colonies and neo-colonies. The internationalism of capital is not met with an internationalism of labour. Racism, and to a certain extent nationalism and religion, play the same role of divide and rule on the global scale as they play on the national stage. Which now brings us to the third feature of racism: political domination.

In places like South Africa political domination is clear-cut. A white minority, through the vicious apartheid system, can dominate the majority. But even within a Western country, racism, by dividing the working people or diverting their attention from the real causes of their misery, necessarily weakens their struggle and results in the domination of the majority by a social minority. Conservative parties in Western Europe, some with even fascist leanings, are often sustained by the votes of the workers especially when such parties directly or indirectly conjure up the spectre of race. Again this is also reflected in international relations. A handful of Western nations continue to dominate a score of nations in Asia, Africa and South America. Despite the fact that the workers in the West are the natural allies of the working people of the 'Third' World, the Western bourgeoisie has not the slightest fear of their workers holding them in check. Yet the Western bourgeoisie has its allies among the dominated nations of Asia, Africa and South America. This is because they have brought up, from among the colonies, semi-colonies and neo-colonies, a native elite imbued with an almost pathological self-hatred and contempt through years of racist cultural engineering. Racism has thus produced an elite endowed with what Frantz Fanon once described as an incurable wish for the permanent identification with the West.

Obscurantism, division, and domination, bring in a fourth feature of racism: exploitation. In other words the first three features are not an end in themselves. The end is more profit. The end result is the appropriation and control of the wealth produced by labour. Capital bleeds labour on both national and international scales. The ideology and practice of racism facilitates that exploitation. For although white workers may be robbed less than black workers, the fact remains that they are all robbed. Otherwise where would profit come from? Surplus value which goes to profit rightfully belongs to labour, and yet labour does not get it all. So between the robbed less and the robbed more it is simply a case of unequal distribution of loss. But the robbed less, 'happy' with their jobs, job 'security' and better pay, do often identify with capital against other sections of labour frequently racially-defined.

Whenever any section of labour sides with capital no matter the reasons for doing so, capital is happy and gains reprieve to continue robbing them all without any fear of a united front. Thus disunity in the labour front, nationally and internationally, aids the exploitation of labour. The easiest of all the time-honoured tools for bringing about this disunity is direct or indirect appeals to racism. The higest concentration of racism as an ideology of exploitation is still South Africa, but apartheid expresses in crude naked form what is embedded in imperialist capitalism as a whole.

The effect of the accumulation of all those features creates a fifth: oppression. Racism, though an ideology, is not felt as a mental or spiritual abstraction. It is felt in the flesh, in the very practice of daily living. The wounds in the flesh of the police violence concentrated on a section of the population identifiable by their colour or religion or both are easier to see. Easier to see?

One of the worst effects of racism is the way it numbs human sensibility. Horrendous things can be done to a section of the population without other sections registering the horror, because their feelings have been numbed to a point where they are unable to see, or hear, what is in front of their eyes and ears. In Western countries, this can be seen in white indifference to police brutality against black people. Internationally, it can be seen in the way advanced capitalist nations can so easily use 'Third' World countries for experiments in new types of medicines and weapons; or as dumping ground for dangerous chemicals and nuclear waste. The question has been asked: if Japan had been white in the European sense, would the USA have been so ready to drop the bomb as it did at Hiroshima and Nagasaki? As it is today, Japan has been made an 'honorary' white, Western, almost European, country on account of its wealth. Hitler used the weapon of racism to numb Nazi Germany into not seeing the crimes against humanity. European nations used the same weapon to make their people not see the crime committed against Africa during the years of the slave trade and slavery and the colonialist occupation of Africa.

Institutional racism permeating many educational, social, and political structures of the West has ended up affecting the general consciousness in society. Personal relationships, feelings, attitudes, values, outlook, self-perception and perception of others, even in the everyday acts of daily living, become affected by racism. Racist values become the norm innocently passed on in the family and in other formative social circles. In fact, so long and so much has racism been part of the imagination and practices of the West that some people are often tempted to see racism as the foundation of all the social evils of the West. The history of capitalism, from the merchant and industrial capital to the finance capital of the imperialist era, gives credence to this interpretation of history and politics. For racism has indeed been part and parcel of slavery, colonialism and now, neo-colonialism.

Those fighting racism must never forget that racism, no matter how all-pervasive, is nevertheless an ideology founded on an economic system of exploitation and social oppression and today this is imperialist capitalism. Equally they must never forget that its victims live its effects hourly, daily, weekly, monthly, all the year round on their bodies, in their bellies, in their minds, in their houses and in the streets. Racism is a psychological, cultural, political, and economic reality and not some disembodied abstraction. The economic, political, cultural and psychological empowerment of the social victims of racism as part of the overall struggle against the roots of racism is the only way of defeating it. The alternative is the continued threat to the peace of humankind. .

The question then arises: is there a connection between racism and the issues of peace in the world today? Yes. For racism, as we have seen, is one of the weapons used against the possible peace of millions of working people in the world. Racism we have argued is meant to, and inevitably has the effect of, stemming the tide of a determined and united struggle of a proud and confident people. Racism is meant to scatter, confuse, and weaken resistance, prevent it, if you like, from reaching the stage of demanding and effecting revolutionary changes in the status quo. Racism is meant to win peace for the exploiting classes and nations. Racism is war against the people by other means.

But when the ideological weapon of racism fails to silence the people, then the ruling bourgeoisie may resort to open arms, to the time-honoured instruments of physical subjugation. The minority, ruling social classes and nations are determined to maintain and defend the status quo of inequality among peoples, nationalities, nations, and regions of the earth by every means at their disposal. The dominant Western economic interests are unanimous, or almost unanimous, in saying or taking a position that seems to say that better the whole world is dead than that the status quo of the starving, homeless and naked millions should radically change.

Racism has been part of all the wars fought in Europe and the world since the seventeenth and eighteenth century. For instance nearly all the wars fought among the British, the French and the Spanish in the eighteenth and nineteenth centuries had to do, among other things, with the slave trade and the slavery of African peoples. The same was true in the American civil war. The First and the Second World Wars were fought over the issue of colonies. When the German imperialist interests lost their African colonies during the First World War, they later tried, through Hitler, to recover them by colonising Europe itself. Note that Nazism had used racism, anti-semitism and anti-blackism, as ideological weapons long before resorting to open arms.

But racist fascism was not invented by Nazi Germany. What of the millions of Africans wantonly killed by the British, the French and the Dutch during the years of slavery and the slave trade? What about the massacres of the same peoples by the same forces in all the colonies? The Jewish holocaust was preceded by an even bigger black holocaust, and we must never forget this. Racism and racist theories to rationalise the wanton massacre of human beings had been voiced, argued out, philosophised about, aestheticised over, by a whole line of respectable artists and intellectuals of the Western world: Hume, Hegel, Carlyle, Froude, and many other image-makers of the Western imagination. The African had to be dehumanised in the mind to explain away the necessity of treating him like a brute in the flesh. But that very racism, grown and nurtured in the system in the seventeenth, eighteenth and nineteenth centuries, struck back in the Europe of the twentieth century by way of Franco, Mussolini, and Hitler. All the methods learnt and practised in the maintenance of the slave trade, slavery, and colonialism, were now being used in the European homelands. The fact is, as has so often been said, that the working class in the imperialist nations will never be fully liberated as human beings without the total liberation of all the peoples of the semi-colonies and neo-colonies. Racism has always been and will always be a threat to world peace. At the very least the victims will never accept any peace and stability based on racism.

Today there is every indication that the third world war will be fought over the re-division of the world, particularly the Third World, among competing giant imperialisms, or in the attempt by the same giant imperialisms to prevent the Third World from controlling its own natural resources. The third world war may well turn out to be a truly 'Third World' war. Most of the trouble spots in the world today lie in Asia, Africa and South America. And in all these, the wars have been waged by, or on behalf of, imperialist interests against the struggles of the peoples for real social changes. The very concept of such arrangements, like the Rapid Deployment Forces, implies the right of the USA or Europe to intervene in Asia, Africa and South America whenever they and they alone deem their interests in those countries to be threatened by external or internal forces. Today the USA has military and nuclear bases in many countries in Asia, Africa and South America. In addition, USA, Britain and France have armed, and continue to arm, many trigger-happy regimes in Asia, Africa and South America. And finally, if one wanted more evidence, there is apartheid South Africa. It is a modern troubleshooter for imperialism in Southern Africa. It is not an accident that the most racist state, in the sense that racism is its ideological foundation, is also the most heavily armed by the West. In South Africa, the ideological offensive of racism and the armed offensive of conventional and nuclear weaponry meet and therefore show, in clear, naked and concrete form, the connection between racism and arms against peace, or rather between racism and war.

It is important therefore that the peace movement in Europe and North America, out of its own interests, fully backs the anti-neo-colonial national and democratic struggles in Asia, Africa and South America. The peace movement, again out of its own interests, should fully support the demands of all the racial minorities in the West and Japan for complete racial equality in law and in institutional practice. It should also back the struggles of all the working people for the control of that which their hands and brains and skills produce. The arms race should be turned into a race to arm the human race against starvation, and homelessness. It should be a race for arming the human race with the means of making us all even more human.

Peace is impossible in a world dominated by imperialism. Peace is impossible in a world guided by the ideology and practice of racism. Hence the struggle for peace in the world must be a concerted struggle against racism and imperialism.

15 *Racism in Literature*

Racism often wages its offensive in print between hardcovers, magazines and newspapers long before it is imprinted on the general consciousness as the basis of personal and institutional practices. The passage of racism into the general practice of the ruling powers is often made smooth by what is agitated for in books, in songs, on the stage, on TV and on the cinema screens. The library in the larger sense of a store house of printed images and whether located in schools, bookshops, public places or in our homes, can become the temple of racism; and literature is often the softest of all the bread and wine served in it.

Racism is the most vicious part of that general ideology that gives rational expression and legitimacy to exploitation, oppression and domination. It does so through obscurantism, that is the masking of the real links between the creation of wealth and of poverty within the nation or in the world; through dividing the dominated on racial lines and therefore weakening the resistance; and through sapping the moral energies of the victims by moulding and remoulding their personalities and their perceptions to make them view the world in accordance with the needs and programmes of the exploiter and the oppressor.

Ideology is the whole system of symbols, images, beliefs, feelings, thoughts, and attitudes by which we explain the world and our place in it. It often comes wrapped up in culture, as cultural practice, but it can also come up wrapped up in books as the conscious programme of a ruling class of a given race or nation. Ideology has a material base and also reflects that material base though with differing degrees of accuracy, depending on which class in that race or nation is controlling the ideology and the material base of that society.

Literature, and particularly imaginative literature, is one of the most subtle and most effective ways by which a given ideology is passed on and received as the norm in the daily practices of our being. Since racism is part of ideology it necessarily finds its rites of passage in the whole field of imaginative literature. So where there is racism, it will be reflected in the literature of that society.

What and how is the connection? All human beings have been infected with the biblical curse of Adam and Eve. You all know the Jewish myth: that Adam and Eve used to dwell in a garden of Eden, an earthly paradise where everything was provided but on condition that they remained in blissful innocence, a phrase for absolute ignorance. Then they were tempted by the desire to know. They wanted to eat from the tree of knowledge. The result? They were thrown out and they were told that henceforth they would live by the sweat of their brow. They were doomed always to struggle for everything by which they lived. Since then, human beings have had to wrestle with nature to get their food, their clothes, their houses, all forms of their material wealth. Their effective struggle with nature has been aided by the development of tools ranging from the simplest stone, knife or axe of the Stone and Iron ages, to the most complicated technologies and gigantic machines of the twentieth century. It has also been aided by co-operation with one another and hence combining their labour in a way that enables them to maximise their general output, often dividing the tasks so that the maker of spears is not at the same time the maker of pots. The biblical curse was a cure after all. It for ever freed human beings from being dependent on the caprices of their environment. In short through the sweat of their brow they developed the means of their emancipation from either kindly or cruel nature. They could now begin to make history. They could now begin to create a human community.

But human beings also struggle among themselves in their interaction with nature and to control that which they have got from their struggles with nature. In short, they struggle to control the labour of others, the tools they use, the ground on which these tools are used and eventually the actual wealth produced during their primary struggle. They have even developed tools and other means of facilitating that social struggle, ranging again from the simplest stone of earlier ages to the most modern weapons of mass destruction.

Out of the two struggles a people evolve into a community with a shared economic and political life. Such a community, by doing similar things over and over again against the background of a shared geography, evolve a common way of life expressed in their languages, in their naming systems, in their dances, songs, religion, art, literature; and in their entire education system. Their culture which is what we are talking about, becomes a kind of social body that carries the values they have evolved in the course of their economic, political and cultural praxis. A given culture carries and transmits concepts of what is right and wrong; what is good or bad; what is beautiful and ugly; and a whole lot of other concepts of honour, courage, glory, heroism – concepts of what in fact they consider to be human. The entire structure of these values often forms the basis of that community's consciousness of itself as a distinct community and the consciousness of its members as belonging to that community rather than any other. It is the basis of their consciousness of who they are in relation to other communities and to the universe, what elsewhere I have called their collective and individual images of self. The selfhood of a community is really their image of who they are.

Their consciousness of who they are may make them look differently at their values, their culture, their political and economic life, at their relationship to nature and to the entire universe. Their economic, political, cultural, and psychological processes are intricately linked to make a complex whole made even more so by the fact that these processes are never at a standstill. Now we can see the importance of who controls any of the processes and particularly the material base of the entire complex whole. But equally well the control of the culture, and hence the values and the self-conception of that community, can effectively retard, accelerate, guide or lead astray their economic and political struggles.

Even within a given community, the social group which controls the wealth also controls the dominant politics and culture of the community. Such a group controls the means of self-definition of that community and it desires to make all the other people view themselves and the world through the set of images it provides. They want to make the entire community, and particularly that section robbed of its wealth, see the world in their way including how to view the whole mechanism of the production and distribution of their wealth. It can never be in the interests of the section controlling the wealth, power and the instruments of self-definition to provide the other sections with the true and correct picture of things as they are. On the contrary, it will use any and every means of obscurantism; of divisions; of shaking their faith in what they actually touch, see, hear, and smell. Racism, or any other form of sectionalism, will be used by the dominant social group to prevent any clear, resolute and united action against its dominant position in that society. It will use each and every myth disguised as education, history, philosophy, religion, aesthetics, to bolster its hegemony on the one hand; and to scatter, confuse and even lead astray the entire resistance hegemony of the other sections.

This is true whether one is talking about the slave owner over the slave in a slave system; the landlord over the serf in a feudal society; the capitalist over the worker in a capitalist society; or the imperialist over the workers of its own and of other countries in a world dominated by imperialism. Such groups try to construct a picture of the universe which bolsters their conception of their place and role in society and in the universe; their conception of the place and the role of all the other people in that universe; and furthermore they will try to sell, by every ideological, educational and cultural means at their disposal, that picture as the eternal, unchanging truth about the nature of the universe.

Racism is part of the ideology of the ruling class of an oppressor nation over all the classes of another nation in another country; or of an oppressor nationality over all the classes of one or more nationalities within the same country. It is inherent in any and every structure of inequality be it slavery, feudalism, capitalism or imperialism in our day. Literature and the general media such as TV, film, radio, newspapers, are merely vehicles for generalising it as the norm in society.

Nobody today talks of slavery as having been necessary for the salvation of the benighted souls of the African. The basis and growth of the slave trade and slavery were economic. C.L.R. James, Eric Williams, W.E.B. DuBois and others have documented the fact that many of the wealthiest cities in Europe were built on the flesh of millions of Africans. At the time of the slave trade and slavery, many academic and scholarly works on everything from history to religious treatises and philosophy were written to rationalise the system on the supposed biological inequalities of the races. Popular and serious works of poetry and fiction were written carrying and reinforcing the images of the inherent inferiority of the oppressed and the inherent superiority of the oppressor. The images were meant to weaken the resistance of the slaves by lowering their conception of their worth and abilities and by raising the spectre of the invincibility of the enemy.

Thus long before direct colonialism had robbed the African of his geography through military conquest and settler economic occupation, of his history through the usurpation of the means of making it, of his culture through alien religions, he had already been robbed of all of these in the literature that was inspired by the slave system or that took that system as the everlasting norm in human relations. Colonialist literature was built on that tradition. The only difference was that during the colonial era the racism in the academic and imaginative literature could now be passed on as gospel truth into the education system. The geography, history, languages, names and all the gods of Europe became the centre of the academic universe of the African child. Racism as a doctrine had left its hiding place in between the hardcovers and was now being paraded as academic brilliance in the colonial classroom.

Literature belongs to those arts that deal directly with the manipulation of images. Its effects can therefore be more poisonous than the poison in the more academic works of learned men like Hegel and Hume and all the other heroes of the imperialist intellectual establishment.

The literature that carried images of Africa and the African ranged from that depicting the self-effacing African as the real human being, or the fun-loving, always smiling type as the more sympathetic being, to that which showed the African resistance fighter as the very reincarnation of cruelty, cowardice, ignorance, stupidity, envy, and even cannibalism. The collaborationist African was glorified. The one who opposed colonialism was vilified. Of course it was not always so directly stated. It was simply the way an author guided the emotions of readers to make them identify with the African who saw no contradictions between himself and colonialism and to distance themselves from the African who argued back, the one who demanded his rightful dues, or the one who, in the banana plantations, plotted against the master. But these were only characters in stories. They were harmless. Harmless?

The cumulative picture could be quite destructive in its psychological effects; we in Africa are today reaping the fruits of that presentation of history in ways that we may not always be able to identify.

The leader of a neo-colonial regime who loses no sleep after annihilating a thousand people in three days; the academic who thrives on writing learned treatises on the backwardness of the African masses and who laughs at every effort of the people to liberate themselves from the neo-colonial bondage; who knows what images of Africa and the African these people might have encountered in the literature of their educational upbringing?

Fortunately for us, history is not one-sided. There is no history which is purely and for all time that of actors and those always acted upon. We already have a glorious history of struggle. The struggle for national liberation has involved a re-evaluation of our culture. The culture of resistance particularly in the songs and poems of the masses has always been part and parcel of that national liberation.

National liberation is a continous process. I believe it is imperative for the progressive teacher, writer, educator, to give African children a picture of themselves in the world consistent with their deepest aspirations for peace, equality and a higher quality of life. The writing of literature, the criticism of literature, the teaching of literature: all these ought to be part and parcel of a total and relentless struggle against the material base of racism which in today's world means capitalism and imperialism.

16 *Her Cook, her Dog*

Karen Blixen's Africa

Up to now, for Western Europe, there have been at least three Africas.

There is first of all the businessman's Africa, or I should say the European hunter after profit. This hunter after profit knows and has always known that Africa is a lucrative ground for his investment. There is a character in Balzac's novel, *Eugénie Grandet*, who is advised by his miserly uncle to go to the tropics to sell human flesh. Charles, the character goes to the tropics, he makes his profit by trading in human beings and of course returns to France, wealthy, a wealthy man who can now marry into nobility. Charles' Africa is the Africa of the European hunter after profit.

Africa has an abundance of raw materials and an abundance of human labour. Like Balzac's Charles, the hunter for profit knows this. It does not matter what, in terms of human beings, the cost is of that profit that enables him to live in palaces and to marry well. His guiding spirit is the rate of profit: whether it is rising or falling. When he looks at Africa it is not to see the human faces of the masses whose poverty and degradation and oppression are the real conditions for his rising rate of profit. No, what he is looking for are conditions of stability, and it does not matter if that stability is founded on the blood and the flesh of millions. It does not matter, if you like, if that stability is founded on the fact that the tongues of millions have been mutilated to make them unable to shout their discontent. Thus, for instance in South Africa today, millions of African workers are being ruthlessly oppressed and silenced, so that the hunter for profit can count his coins in peace and then talk about the aids and loans from the 'developed' world to the developing countries.

The Danish Library Association would render a great service to our mutual understanding if through such anthologies it could bring home to the Danish people that Europe's vaunted development is founded on Africa's underdevelopment; that the food and the water that Europe's hunter for profit eats and drinks is often snatched from the mouths of the hungry and the mouths of the thirsty.

The other kind of Africa is the Africa for the European hunter after pleasure. This is the tourists' Africa. When coming in the plane, by Sabena Airlines, I looked through the current issue of the *Sabena* magazine and came across an article on safari-hunting in Kenya. To the writer of the article, Kenya is completely devoid of human beings. The Kenya in that magazine is a vast animal landscape, ruled over by elephants, lions and leopards. A lot of books about Africa are like that: they cater to the taste of the hunter for pleasure, the hunter after wild game, the tourists.

When human beings traverse that landscape depicted in the tourist literature, it is only as a part of that animal landscape. If you go into many libraries or bookshops to look for books about Africa, you are more likely to find such titles as *Vanishing Africa*, *The Authentic African*, and so on. In the pictures that illustrate the books, such Africans are nearly always naked and they are often photographed with animals to show the harmony with the animal landscape. The hunter for pleasure is really the hunter for profit but on holiday. He does not want to see or face up to the reality that it is the African worker who creates his profit. Hence the literary deathwish for the African engaged in the active struggle against nature and against human degradation.

But there is a third Africa – and for me a most dangerous Africa – beloved by both the hunter for profit and the hunter for pleasure. This is the Africa in European fiction.

The creators of this kind of Africa are best represented by the Danish writer by the name of Karen Blixen, alias Isak Dinesen. Karen Blixen had a farm in Kenya, which formed the basis of her book *Out of Africa*. *Out of Africa* is one of the most dangerous books ever written about Africa, precisely because this Danish writer was obviously gifted with words and dreams. The racism in the book is catching, because it is persuasively put forward as love. But it is the love of a man for a horse or for a pet. She writes: 'When you have caught the rhythm of Africa, you find that it is the same in all her music. What I learned from the game of the country was useful to me with my dealings with the native people.'

What she is really saying is that her knowledge of wild animals gave her a clue to the African mind. I'll give you another example before I finish with this Africa. In the same book, *Out of Africa*, she writes a great deal about her cook, Kamante. But he is described in terms of a pet dog: I quote: 'Kamante could have no idea as to how a dish of ours ought to taste and he was in spite of his conversation and his connection with civilization at heart an arrant Kikuyu rooted in the traditions of his tribe and in his faith in them as the only way of living worthy of a human being. He did at times taste the food he cooked, but with a distrustful face like a witch who takes a sip out of her cauldron. He stuck to the maize-cob of his fathers, even here his intelligence sometimes failed him and he came and offered me a Kikuyu delicacy, a roasted sweet potato, or a lump of sheep's fat, even as a civilized dog who has lived for a long time with people will place a bone on the floor before you as a present.'

So to Karen Blixen, Kamante is comparable to a civilised dog that has lived long with human beings, Europeans of course.

It might be argued that the racist views in the book, *Out of Africa*, were accidental; that they were the views of a young romantic but ignorant lady of an aristocracy in decline. But in her other book *Shadows in the Grass* published in 1960 when Karen Blixen was already aged and when a number of African countries were getting their independence, she repeated her racist views even more emphatically:

'The dark nations of Africa, strikingly precocious as young children, seemed to come to a standstill in their mental growth at different ages. The Kikuyu, Kawirondo and Wakambo, the people who worked for me on the farm, in early childhood were far ahead of white children of the same age, but they stopped quite suddenly at a stage corresponding to that of a European child of nine. The Somali had got further and had all the mentality of boys of our own race at the age 13 to 17.'

In the same book she describes how in her old age in Denmark, African people would appear to her in dreams. But they came to her disguised as animals, dwarf elephants, bats, leopards and jackals.

I could quote more passages of a similar nature but those will do.

Karen Blixen is, of course, entitled to her views, however sickening. But Karen Blixen is more than this. She is a European phenomenon. To Western Europe she is a saint, a literary saint, and she has been canonised as such. She embodies the great racist myth at the heart of the Western bourgeois civilisation. She is the authority on Africa and many European and American children are brought up on Karen Blixen.

So by bringing to the Danish people this type of anthology where African writers are talking about themselves and their conditions, the Danish Library Association is doing a tremendous service in rectifying the harm done to Africa by the likes of Karen Blixen, who was really in effect a spokeswoman for the hunter for gold and the hunter for pleasure.

17 *Biggles, Mau Mau and I*

I met Squadron-Leader James Bigglesworth, DSO DFC MC, at one time of the Royal Flying Corps, later The Royal Air Force, and known to his readers as simply Biggles, at Alliance High School, in Kenya, back in 1956. I followed his every adventure in Europe, Asia and Africa. *Biggles and Co*; *Biggles in Spain*; *Biggles Flies East*: *Biggles in the Orient*; *Biggles Defies the Swastika*; *Biggles Hunts Big Game*; Biggles here, Biggles there, Biggles everywhere: the shelves in the school library could not have enough of Biggles to satisfy the thirst and hunger for adventure of a sixteen-year-old boy from the rural areas of Kenya. Through him I could even fly an aeroplane and travel to all those places and emerge triumphant against all those crooks – mostly Germans, at least not English – bent on ruining the world as made by Pax Brittanica. Britain ruled the waves, earth and sky, bringing about the best of all possible worlds, and all that was now needed was the resolve of her brave sons to police the new world order and defeat any evil that threatened it. These braves had done so during both the First and Second World Wars and Biggles symbolised this breed of tough Englishmen, the breed of the happy few, whose long line of selfless service went back to the founders of the empire.

I must say that even then Biggles never captured my whole hearted affection the way Stevenson's creations in *Treasure Island* or Dickens' in *Oliver Twist* had done. Jim Hawkins; Long John Silver; Oliver Twist: these characters had become my cherished companions and lines like 'Yo ho and a bottle of rum/Sixteen men on a dead man's chest . . .' or 'Please sir can I have some more', kept on intruding in my mind like one's favourite tunes. I cannot for instance remember the number of times I read and reread *Treasure Island*. In the case of the Biggles series, there were no memorable lines or episodes or images. Not a single title could stand the test of a second read. Nevertheless there was a way in which more than Stevenson's Jim Hawkins or Dickens' Oliver Twist, Biggles, the creation of Captain W.E. Johns belonged to the school and my world.

It was a colonial school in a colonial world. The school, founded by an Alliance of protestant Missions way back in the thirties, was the leading elitist school for African children. Its motto, 'Strong to Serve', expressed the ideals of the school: to produce leaders who of course, had the necessary character and knowledge to faithfully but intelligently serve King and Empire. It was a boarding school run on military lines. Wake up in the morning at five. Make beds. Cold showers. Clean the compound. Parade. Marching band of bugles, trumpets and drums. Raise the British flag. Inspection for cleanliness with marks awarded to the various residential dormitories. Chapel. Organ or piano music. 'Lead kindly light amidst the encircling gloom, lead thou me on'. Boy scouts. Mountain climbing. Sports. Anything that went to build physical health, moral character and sound intellect, the three most important arms against the gloom. It was a school where Kipling's poem 'If' was so very important. And of course Shakespeare. But Biggles? Oh yes, Biggles. He was on a mission to defeat all those forces that were part of the gloom. The flag which we saluted every day accompanied by bugles, trumpets and drums, and 'God Save the Queen, Long to reign over us', was central to the Biggles enterprise. Biggles' loyalty was first and foremost to the flag. Our school was bringing up young men for whom loyalty to God and to the flag would be two sides of the same coin. The enemies of the Empire whether the French, the Germans or the Russians would also be our enemies.

The Germans especially were already familiar villains in our school history lessons. Had they not tried to remove the British from East Africa? And remember the many Kenyans who had died in both the First and Second World War fighting against those villains? In our school the teachers always talked about the rigid teutonic mentality against of course the more flexible and morally superior English character. Biggles in action represented this ideal, the English character of Kipling's 'If'. So did the school. The headmaster led in the recitation of the poem 'If'. When he came to the last lines of the poem, he would pause, look at the assembled eyes and ears and then, with a trembling voice, he would make the dramatic call: 'and what is more, you'll be a man, my son'. Kenyan sons of Kipling aspiring to graduate as real British men. Oh, we the happy few. Some of the teachers saw themselves as part of this heroic few. Had they not given up life in an Engish climate to bring light to the dark corners of the Empire? Some of the teachers had seen action in the Second World War. One in the Royal Air Force. The Royal Air Force? That should have alerted me, should have made Biggles my enemy.

I came from a large peasant family in Limuru. The school, ten miles away, was the furthest I had been away from home. Opposite the African reserves at Limuru were the Kenya Highlands, since 1895 occupied by British settlers determined to turn Kenya into a White Man's country. The school grounds were also adjacent to huge farms also owned by white settlers. Among these settlers were those soldiers who had fought in the First and Second World War. But the Kenyan Africans who had been active in the same wars were part of the landless and jobless majority in the cities and rural areas. The white soldiers had the votes; the Kenyan Africans did not. The white soldiers were the beneficiaries of British colonial presence. The African soldiers rejected their destiny as hewers of wood and joined the Mau Mau guerrilla army. Among these was Dedan Kīmathi who later became the supreme leader of the guerrilla army. The Mau Mau war to oust the British from Kenya broke out in 1952, the year of the Queen Elizabeth's accession to the throne; and of Jomo Kenyatta's arrest. In 1954 my elder brother ran to the mountains to join the Mau Mau guerrilla army. In the three years from 1953 to 1956, the year of Kīmathi's capture, the Mau Mau forces were at their strongest, constituting a parallel government authority in the land. What actually broke the back of Mau Mau in the mountains was the intensive bombing by the Royal Air Force. Mau Mau had no reply to the terror from the sky. My brother, who survived the war, still talks with awe of the bombings.

So in reading Biggles in the years 1955 and 1956, I was involved in a drama of contradictions. Biggles, the flying ace and squadron leader of the Royal Air Force, could have been dropping bombs on my own brother in the forests of Mount Kenya. Or he could have been sent by Raymond of Scotland Yard to ferret out those who were plotting against the British Empire in Kenya. Either way he would have been pitted against my own brother who, amidst all the fighting in the forest, still found time to send messages to me to cling to education no matter what happened to him. In the forests they, who were so imbued with Kenya nationalist patriotism, had celebrated my being accepted into the same Alliance High School where I was to meet Biggles, an imaginary character so imbued with a sense of British patriotism. This may have explained the distance between me and Biggles. He was nothing but English. Englishness represented a human ideal; and the human ideal ended in the Englishness of his being and actions and motives.

This was also the basis of the gender and racist definition of the world. In the world of Biggles women do not really exist. After all empire-building and its defence was a masculine feat, to be applauded by admiring, but delicate, white females.

The world was a racial hierarchy of the English, the whites and the rest of malekind. All white people were equal in relation to the non-European universe but the English were more equal than the other whites.

A good example is in the description of the Anglo-German struggle and their non-European allies in *Biggles Flies East*. This book introduces Biggles' German adversary, Hauptmann Erich von Stalhein. There is a kind of admiration of this particular German, he is the German Biggles if that were possible; he does for the German side the kind of spectacular feats of courage and daring that Biggles does for the British side. At one time Biggles after being forced to land somewhere in the Middle East, suddenly sees von Stalhein conferring with some Arabs:

> His astonishment gave way to curiosity and then to intense interest as he watched the scene. It seemed to him that von Stalhein, from his actions, was exhorting the Arabs to do something, something they were either disinclined to do, or about which they were divided in their opinions. But after a time it became apparent that the more powerful personality of the white man was making itself felt, and in the end there was a general murmur of assent . . .

Note that in being made to arrive at that conclusion by the author, Biggles is not described as having heard a single word spoken, or deciphered the actual arguments. But from where he is well hidden he can still discern that whiteness is an important ingredient of the German's make-up.

But of course in the white zone itself the English character occupies the whitest spot. In *Biggles Hunts Big Game*, the hero goes to Africa to root out some crooks who are ruining the post-war world of the victorious British and their allies by printing fake currencies. The criminal mastermind is of some European stock but he is of course being helped by African-American crooks dressed like real natives of the African jungle. In Cairo before both hero and villain board a plane for Kudinga in Central Africa, Biggles is able to observe the criminal mastermind whom he describes as being very well-dressed with a suit of European cut.

> His complexion was so pale that at first, from a distance, Biggles took him to be a pure European; but as a result of a more prolonged scrutiny he changed his mind, and concluded that the smooth, olive-tint was almost certainly that of an Euroasian, or at any rate a European with more than a trace of mid-eastern blood in his veins – a guess that was supported by the flash of a diamond tie-pin of a size so vulgar that no British visitor would be likely to wear it at such a time and place.

Nearly all the books in the Biggles series are shot through and through with this racial and gender demarcation of the universe and in this it is very much in line with all the racist popular literature – Rider Haggard, John Buchan, Nicholas Monsarrat for instance – that glorified imperialism and the deeds of its British actors while vilifying those of its opponents be they from rival imperialisms or from the native resistance like the Mau Mau of which my own brother was an active agent.

What, then, made me read all the Biggles then available in the school? I had discovered literature, written literature. I had seen a library for the first time in my life. Books. Books everywhere. Book, any book, was magic to me. This was a time when I looked forward to being able to read all the books that had ever been published. I was at an age when I could happily read Emily Brontë and Tolstoy alongside John Buchan and Rider Haggard and enjoy them equally. But it was also a stage in my life when what was most important in literature was the story and the element of what happens next. And this the Biggles books had in plenty. The Biggles series were full of actions, intrigues, thrills, twists, surprises and a very simple morality of right against wrong, angels against devils, with the good always triumphant. It was adventure all the way, on land and in the sky. And what is more one did not have to read more than fifty pages before one was in the thick of the action. They were the kind of books that told a young man: once you start reading me, you will not put me down. It was the strong action which made one forget, or swallow, all the racist epithets of the narratives. The books did not invite meditation; just the involvement in the actions of the hero and his band of faithfuls, Ginger, Algy and Bertie.

They were a boy's books really. I could never think of Biggles as an adult. He learnt to fly at the age of seventeen as described in *Biggles Learns to Fly* and he remained just that: an adolescent, a boy scout, and this was probably the image that beckoned the youth from the the rural area of a basically oral society. Biggles was a boy, daring to try, never giving up, stretching the boundaries of what was credible, it is true, but still inviting the boy readers to join in the adventure, albeit in a race-coloured universe of the English, the Whites and the rest of us.

18 Black Power in Britain

If I could make every black person read one book on the history of black people in the West, that would have to be C.L.R. James's, *The Black Jacobins*. The second would be Eric Williams's *Capitalism and Slavery*. To that list I will now add, particularly for people in Britain, Peter Fryer's *Staying Power: The History of Black People in Britain*.

It opens with a startling declaration: 'there were Africans in Britain before the English came here.' It then goes on to unearth a mass of details to show that there has been a continuous black presence in this country for the last four or five hundred years or, at least, since the sixteenth century. They were brought here often against their will, to serve this country. This fact has also been vividly captured by a twelve-year-old resident of Hackney, Brian Collins, in a recent poem, 'Our Country Now', to be found in a collection of poems by London school students titled, *Our City*, and published by Young World Books in 1984 to mark the Year of Anti-Racism.

Our Country Now

My home is Grenada
My home is London
One day long ago
My brothers came from the islands.
We worked on the buses
We worked in the hospitals
We worked on the railways
We were asked over here
To make Britain work again.

142

We sweated long hours
Every day and every night,
Hard work all our lives.
We say we built Britain
We bled for our children's children,
This is our home.
I am part of Grenada
I am part of London
My brothers are part of England
For all time,
Our country now.

By their very presence here, these people always brought with them the very issues which were being argued out, with words or blows or both, in the plantations and goldmines of the British Empire. Mother England could afford to look benign and benevolent and even pretend that those things happened only in the outposts of the Empire or in the United States of America. Racism was something peculiar to South Africa and the USA, conveniently forgetting that these were creations of the British colonial genius.

It has taken the shrinking of the Empire in the fifties and sixties, the racist immigration laws of the sixties and seventies, and the Black people's resistance to institutional and personal discrimination to bring the issues to the doors and sitting rooms of every inhabitant of this country. The riots of the eighties, the violence unleashed against Black people, and the activities of National Front-type organisations, made it abundantly clear that racism was not necessarily a monopoly of the USA and South Africa. Racism no longer resided only 'out there' in the outsposts of the Empire but also here in the original belly of the beast.

In fact 'racism has been an integral part of the growth of capitalism' from its inception in the seventeenth- and eighteenth-century slave trade, the plantation slavery, and the industrial revolution that followed the slave products of sugar, cotton and tobacco through to nineteenth-century laissez-faire capitalism and the domination of imperialist finance capital of the colonial and neo-colonial era. Capitalism, it has been said and correctly so; came to the world dripping with blood. This blood was mostly of Asian and African peoples.

Thus the effects of racism are not lived through as disembodied capital but as a reality. Its victims, particularly those of African and Asian origins, live it daily, hourly, in their places of work, in the streets, in their homes and in their very beings. Racism as a felt experience is brilliantly captured in the works of the young writers, mostly born and brought up here in Britain, in that collection of poems, *Our City*, that I have already referred to. A poem by Kashim Chowdhury, a twelve-year-old from Spitalfields, captures the general mood of the haunting presence of impending violence experienced by the young living in Britain today:

Our City

I live in London
Where racism turns to violence.
My family are struggling
When news comes of bills going up.
Where I live
The streets are dirty
With rubbish thrown out that is stinking.

The housing is bad
Because burglars could get in
And then we turn sad.
We are frightened to go out at night
Just in case we are hauled into a fight.

We wake up at dawn again
And give a big yawn.
We've got to go to school through a dark tunnel
Where we're sure there's got to be trouble.
We get most of the bullying in school,
But there's nothing I could do.

When it gets dark
White bullies come out with dogs that bark
With knives that glow in the dark,
We're sure we're going to be struck.

The weather is usually cloudy,

Sometimes it turns rainy.
Prices of food go up day by day,
Which makes our simply enjoying life go away.

The answer to that reality so graphically described by Chowdhury is given by another youth, Paul Lehane (eleven years old), in the same collection and in just two lines at the end of his poem on the city:

Harmony is what we want
But we'll have to fight for it.

Fight for it. Struggle for it! Not least of the significance of the testimony in *Staying Power* is the fact that the book is written by a white person; and, according to him, it was a chance remark during the 1981 riots which finally led him to start this massive compilation of data that grew into such a gripping story of black people's presence and their contribution in Britain over so many years. In other words, it was an act of resistance to racism by its bruised recipients which prompted him to attempt a general re-evaluation of the black presence in Britain.

The book itself is, in part, a record of that resistance and of the staying power of black people we saw described in Brian Collins' poem. Many brilliant minds jump out of its pages to illuminate our perception of the history of Britain and its dialectical link to that of an Empire now reborn as neo-colonies: Ottobah Cugoano, Olaudah Equiano, William Davidson, Robert Wedderburn, William Cuffy, Mary Seacole, and many others right up to the present day likes of George Padmore and C.L.R. James. We should know their stories.

But the real staying power is that of the struggles of labour, black labour and other people's labour, ordinary men and women whose names will never appear in history text-books. It is their struggles in Britain, which added to those of the national liberation efforts of their counterparts in Asia, Africa and the Caribbean which have put racism on the agenda in the twentieth century, calling out loudly for immediate solutions.

19 *Many Years Walk to Freedom*

Welcome Home Mandela!

Watched by thousands who had gathered in Cape Town to witness the miracle and by millions of others around the world via television, Mandela walked hand in hand with his wife, Winnie, to a personal freedom and triumph. He was writing the date – February 11, 1990 – into world history. And when he spoke he brought joy as he publicly reaffirmed his belief in the people of South Africa and in the principles for which he had been prepared to die – a democratic, nonracial and unitary South Africa.

Millions had waited for this event over many years but intensely more so in the few days preceeding it, a fact best symbolised by a nine-year-old girl, Lashambi, and her mother, Njeeri wa Ndūng'ū. From the age of six Lashambi had collected every newspaper and magazine article and pictures of Nelson and Winnie Mandela she could get. The door and walls of her bedroom were literally pasted with the Mandelas under a big heading: Free Mandela. For years she had urged her mother, who she of course thought could move mountains, to simply telephone the South African Presidents and demand the release of Mandela. If her mother could intervene with school Presidents, why not with all Presidents? When nine days earlier F. W. De Klerk had announced that Mandela would be free, she greeted the news by jumping up and down and urging her mother: 'Let's make a big card and send it to Mandela. Welcome Home, Baaba Mandela, we will say.' Lashambi and her mother, Njeeri, live in Newark, NJ, USA. In 1963 when Mandela was jailed for life, the mother, who was born in Mang'u, Kenya, had been only seven years old. Now she and her nine-year-old daughter were waiting for Mandela. Quite clearly Mandela has been in the minds of and hearts of several generations – not only in Africa but in many parts of the world, in the minds and hearts of all who value human freedom. Thousands had marched for his release in virtually every city and village in the world. Streets had been named after him. Music in his name was selling in millions of records. Books had been written about him. Sculptors and painters too had tried to capture the image of this prisoner of apartheid. The whole world had been waiting for Mandela.

Why have Mandela's name and personality captivated so many people? He was not the only prisoner for life. Indeed, many political detainees have died in the prisons of South Africa. Others have been massacred before the eyes of the world: Sharpeville in the sixties; Soweto in the seventies. In fact, for the black people of South Africa the whole country has been one vast jailhouse. This was particularly so in the years of pass laws and passbooks.

The most compelling thing about Mandela is how he endured those years of solitary confinement and other tortures without ever surrendering to the racist vampires. In him people see the infinite capacity of the human spirit to resist and to conquer. Hurrah for the spirit of resistance! Do we not for the same reason identify in literature with characters like Prometheus? And in history with people like Paul Robeson, Kwame Nkrumah, Ho Chi Minh, Nat Turner, Toussaint L'Overture, Kenyan freedom fighter Dedan Kīmathi, Zimbabwean resistance leader Mbuya Nehanda, and martyred Chilean poet and singer Victor Jara?

All these figures are heroic because they reflect more intensely in their individual souls the souls of their community. Their uniqueness is the uniqueness of the historical moment. They make history even as history makes them. They are torches that blaze out new paths. Such a torch has been set alight by the fire of the masses, and every time it seems to fade, the great ones turn to their people for more energy. Mandela has been such a torch for the South African people. The black people of South Africa are reflected in Mandela.

In Mandela the people of the world have really been applauding the courage, the endurance, the resistance and spirit of the South African masses. The people of the world, particularly Africans and those of African descent outside Africa, have in turn seen themselves reflected in the struggling South African masses. Or put another way, Mandela is to black South Africa's struggles what black South Africa's struggles are to the democratic forces of the world in the twentieth century. Indeed, South Africa is a mirror of the modern world in its emergence over the last four hundred years.

A large claim? Not really. When Vasco da Gama landed at the Cape of Good Hope in 1498, he not only found for Western Europe an easier route to India's riches, he also started the long era of Africa's unequal and unwilling partnership in the development of Europe and the newly discovered Americas. Europe's two greatest political economists and philosophers, Adam Smith and Karl Marx, agree in their writings that the 'discovery' of the sea route to India via South Africa and of the continent of America were the two most important events in the emergence, growth and development of post-Renaissance Europe. Adam Smith called them 'the two greatest and most important events in the history of mankind'; Karl Marx described them as opening up 'fresh ground for the rising bourgeoisie' and as giving to trade, commerce and industry 'an impulse never before known'.

South Africa, though farthest removed from Europe, became Europe's gateway to the heart of the continent. In a world context, South Africa also became the knot that tied together the diverse histories and fortunes of Asia, Europe and America. Like the rest of the continent, South Africa saw her people hunted down and carried away as slaves. Their labour was used to develop what later became the United States, and profits from the sale of their bodies as commodities became part of the capital that authorities like W.E.B. DuBois, C.L.R. James and Eric Williams have proved was the basis of Western Europe's nineteenth-century industrial takeoff.

From 1652, when first the Dutch and French and finally the British settlers streamed into South Africa and began forcibly taking land from the Africans, to the nineteenth century (when the whole country became first a British colony and then a neo-colony supervised by a white minority), the gold, diamonds and minerals of South Africa were used to develop Western European industries – and later America's, too – and for the building of enormous gold reserves. Is there any bank, financial institution or industry of any significant size in Western Europe, the US and Japan that is not indebted to the gold and diamonds of South Africa?

The majority of the industries inside South Africa are branches, subsidiaries or partners of those in the West, and their enormous profits have been clearly rooted in the slave wages of black workers and in the general poverty of the majority guaranteed by the cruel system of *apartheid*. The South African economy is inextricably tied to that of the West. So it's not surprising that Britain and the United States have been hostile to calls for economic boycotts. To respond to such calls would in reality be to institute boycotts against themselves. In fact, boycott calls began to have some kind of effect only when the democratic forces in the US realised that the pillars of *apartheid* were right at their doorstep. The USA then started to consider economic sanctions and to pressure its business community to co-operate.

In the South African system, people see the bitter fruition in this century of at least five forces that have bedeviled the real development of human beings: classical colonialism, neo-colonialsm, slave wages, racism and the usurpation of the people's sovereignty through the denial of democracy. But black South Africans do not present the picture of endlessly helpless victims of superior forces. Their history presents a people who have pioneered in the struggle for communal survival, national liberation and social emancipation. The success of their resistance can be measured more accurately by juxtaposing their history with that of the other major areas invaded by European settlers in the seventeenth and eighteenth centuries. In the Americas, Canada and Australia, Europeans virtually wiped out the native populations, whereas the ferocity of black South Africans' resistance blunted the determined efforts of European settlers to annihilate them. Shaka, the great king of the Zulu, is possibly the best known of all the leaders of pre-twentieth-century resistance in Africa, and his name continues to inspire liberation efforts.

Black South Africa has had to pay a high price for its resistance. From Shaka to Mandela, its people have experienced one massacre after another at the hands of Europeans. The Sharpeville and Soweto massacres make African people recall other massacres in colonial African history – Hola Camp in Kenya, Miriyamu in Mozambique, Algiers in Algeria. But the black people of South Africa have never given up hope, not even when others, who began organised struggles years after theirs, have raised national flags and sung national anthems.

There have been other pioneering successes in black South Africa.

The African National Congress, formed in 1912, is one of the oldest of modern political parties in Africa. The ANC can be described as the father and mother of all the other African liberation movements. Its anthem, 'Nkosi Sikelele Africa' [God Bless Africa], is the nearest thing to a pan-African internationale, and even today it is the national anthem of Tanzania and Zimbabwe. Furthermore, Africa is not the only beneficiary of the pioneering liberation struggles of the black South African people. Remember that Mahatma Gandhi of India started his political activism in South Africa. And the independence of India in 1948 had quite an impact on independence movements throughout the rest of Asia and Africa.

In literature too: the names of Thomas Mofolo, Vilikazi, Peter Abrahams, Eskia Mphahlele, Alex la Guma, Mazisi Kunene, Miriam Tlali to mention just a few are virtually inseparable from the development of literature in the rest of the continent.

But the one thing that makes every African, every black person in the world, see him/herself reflected in the history of the black South African people – and therefore of Mandela – is the titanic fight against racism and the colour line, once described by W.E.B. DuBois as *the* problem of the twentieth century. Racial oppression carries within it many denials – economic, political, cultural and psychological. Who does not see him/herself reflected in that mirror?

South Africa is me. South Africa is you. South Africa is all the black people of the earth. South Africa is all the workers of the world. South Africa is humanity in a struggle to save itself. If that struggle for the recovery of a sense of human community is led by South Africa's masses through their political organisations, like the South African Communist Party, the ANC and the Pan-African Congress, it is equally true that Nelson Mandela has been its leading symbol. He has firmly held aloft the mirror in which the twentieth century has been looking at itself.

One hopes that his release, coming as it does in the closing decade of the twentieth century, amid so many changes taking place in the power map of the world and the cries everywhere for power to the people, will be only a short step to the liberation of the black South African people so that they can control their economy, their politics and their culture. Whether they achieve that kind of empowerment or not will depend on the extent to which they can resist being pressured by the West to accept the Kenya solution.

In 1962, Jomo Kenyatta was released from eight years in prison, and he proceeded to negotiate away everything that the Mau Mau armed struggle had fought for. Colonial structures were left intact, and today Kenya under successor Daniel arap Moi is one of the most repressive states in the world, a neo-colony completely and pathetically dependent on the West. Kenyatta lost on the negotiating table what had already been won on the battlefield by the Kenyan people.

Black South Africa cannot accept, or indeed afford, the replacement of the 1910 neo-colonial arrangement under white-minority supervision by a 1990s refined neo-colonial arrangement to be run by a black minority. The history of the last four hundred years calls upon them to overthrow forever and completely the triple burdens of colonialism, neo-colonialism and racial oppression and to start on a genuine march toward social justice for all.

Mandela's release is his own victory and the victory of the ANC and the other liberation movements; of the black South African people and of all black and African peoples; and of all the lovers of human freedom. Now that Mandela is free, people of the world must redouble the support for liberation movements in their demands for independence and freedom.

Perhaps the nine-year-old girl was so excited about Mandela's release because in it she caught a glimpse of tomorrow – as it will be created by a generation determined to ensure that the twenty-first century will be the century of Africa and of all other exploited and oppressed people of the earth.

IV

Matigari,
Dreams &
Nightmares

20 Life, Literature & a Longing for Home

Have you ever had the sensation of being in two places at the same time? Tomorrow for instance I am returning to England from New England after five months of teaching literature and politics for the English and Comparative Literature Departments at Yale University in New Haven, not too far from New London.

The colleges are a replica of Oxford, down to the colour of the stones. They were built during the Depression by imported Italian craftsmen who left their signatures on the roofs and walls of the gothic architecture by way of gargoyles – with faces mocking at scholarship.

The first student was a Jacob Heminway, enrolled in March 1702, paving the way for a long line of others who would be instructed in the Arts and Sciences and 'fitted for public Employment both in Church and Civil State'. Until the sixties and seventies this long line hardly included Blacks and women. Today it is co-educational and multiracial, although Blacks are still a minority.

Like the other Ivy League colleges Yale attracts very good students and its graduates readily find employment in all sorts of places and positions. One of its law graduates has even found his way to the highest position in Civil State. His name is George Bush, and he has employed another Yalian, D. Alan Bromley, as his national adviser in the sciences and technology.

*

Writers are supposed to have an opinion on everything from geography, history, physics and chemistry to the fate of humankind.

154

Recently I attended a workshop in Stockholm on Development ment Assistance for the Nineties. I gave a paper on 'The Impact of Donors and Development Assistance on the Recipient Cultures'.

I joined the other Africans present in taking a position which was different from that of the expert from the World Bank who kept on citing Kenya, Malawi, Cameroon, and Ivory Coast – all repressive, all subservient to the West – as the success stories of IMF Africa.

These were experts on micro and macroeconomics who had drawn complicated graphs and figures and quoted statistics, and were supposed to understand each other's languages.

When later during a boatride in the Stockholm waters I met Per Wästberg, the Swedish novelist and former President of International PEN, I suddenly realised how glad I was simply to talk shop with another writer.

Wästberg is the author of *Eldens Skugga* (*The Shadows of Fire*) and *Bergets Kalla* (*Source of the Mountain*), and numerous other articles and books on Africa. As the boat moved towards the centre of Stockholm he talked about the places of his childhood which were also the landscape of a number of his novels set in Stockholm.

Do you see that statue? It is Gustaf III, the King of Sweden, murdered in 1792 at a masquerade ball at Stockholm opera. Many people have drawn parallels between his murder and that of Olof Palme. And there he suddenly stopped, obviously reliving the pain and other memories for a person who was not only his country's loved premier but also a personal and family friend.

What was emerging was Wästberg's love of the physical and social landscape of his upbringing as a citizen and as a writer, and I felt slightly overwhelmed by a sense of my own exile from Kenya.

For the last six years I have lived in Islington, and this self-contained urban village near the heart of London has become a kind of second home. My novel, *Matigari*, was written in Gĩkũyũ at 85c Noel Road which makes me identify with Islington all the more. When I was invited to Yale last year I hesitated.

Would this not drive me even farther away from Kenya and Africa? So as soon as I landed in New Haven in mid-January, I threw myself into writing a filmscript, *Kariũki*, for a project involving film-makers from Zimbabwe, Tanzania, Mozambique, Zambia and Sweden.

Writing has always been my way of reconnecting myself to the landscape of my birth and upbringing. For a few weeks I completely shut out New Haven from my consciousness. I was back in Africa of the twenties and thirties. I lived its landscape, its rivers, its history and only after this imaginative return did I wake up to where I was – New Haven, Connecticut.

I was living in the Taft apartments on College Street facing Bishop Tutu's corner. Bishop Tutu in Yale? In fact the South Africa issue is all around Yale. My students talk about it. And outside the offices of the President of Yale are shacks made of cardboard, paper and sacks. These were built by the students and maintained there as a constant reminder that Yale should divest itself of interests in South Africa.

Yale has one of the best libraries in the United States. I one day walk through the corridors of its silence. I tiptoe to the section which I have been told contains nearly all the newspapers in the world. I go for the Kenya newspapers which I have not seen for a long time.

It was early March. And what do I see staring at me from the pages of the newspaper? President Moi of Kenya at a public meeting denouncing me and claiming that I was in Sudan, obviously plotting against him. We'll talk of being in two places at the same time. I have never been to Sudan.

I should not have worried about being very far from Kenya. On arrival in New Haven, one of the earliest internal letters I get is from the director of the programme of African Languages at Yale written in perfect Gĩkũyũ. She is an American.

Kiswahili, Yoruba, Hausa and Zulu are taught at Yale and this summer they are introducing Gĩkũyũ and Shona. The programme has quantities of teaching material and books in Gĩkũyũ and Kiswahili. One of the 24 graduate students in my seminar on literature and politics has studied Kiswahili, Gĩkũyũ, Hausa, on top of her knowledge of European languages.

She is one among the 10 students admitted every year into the graduate programme of the Comparative Literature Department from more than a hundred applicants. When I had dinner with one of the editors of the prestigious *Yale Journal of Criticism* I tried to get out of her request that I contribute an article by telling her that I only wrote in Gĩkũyũ. She looked me in the eye and said: write in Gĩkũyũ. We shall publish it.

I have enjoyed being in the classroom again after more than six years. Seminars can be very stimulating although very demanding. The students with their passionate debates, quarrels, shoutings, and arguments make me feel at home, and I begin looking forward to every seminar. But of course I am daily struck by the absurdity of the situation. In my own country I was banned from teaching at the university, or in any school.

The kind of issues we are raising in the classrooms of Yale would land all of us in prison for anything between one and ten years. I tell the students this, and they look amazed since what we are saying is nothing particularly revolutionary. We are only looking at the relevance of fiction to the facts of life!

Every time I give a public reading from the English translation of my novel, *Matigari*, I am in two minds about telling the story behind its being banned in Kenya in its Gĩkũyũ original. But the story does illustrate the absurdity of a writer's situation in a repressive state. The novel was first published in Kenya in October 1986. Soon after, reports reached President Moi that peasants in Central Kenya were talking about a man called Matigari who was going round the country demanding truth and justice. Moi ordered the man's immediate arrest.

The police reported that Matigari was only a character in a book. Still in February 1987 *Matigari* was 'arrested' and removed from all the bookshops in Nairobi and from the publisher's warehouse. Which reminds me that my previous novel in Gĩkũyũ, *Devil On the Cross*, had met a similar fate at Kamĩtĩ Maximum Security Prison in 1978. But that was only written on toilet paper and it was later returned to me as harmless. Well, Matigari seems to be made of sterner stuff.

A writer inhabits two places at the same time: the land of facts and that of fiction. But in a neo-colonial situation fiction seems to be more real than the absurdity of the factual world of a dictator. The world of a dictator has an element of pure fantasy. He will kill, jail, and drive hundreds into exile and imagine that he is actually loved for it.

One of course wishes that the world of a dictator was only

confined to hardcovers. But it isn't and a dictator will even think of dragging characters from fiction into the streets. Perhaps that proves the relevance of literature to life. Or put it this way: dictators are the best students of literature. Or the most serious! This does not mean that they have learned anything from either literature or history.

21 *Matigari,*
& the Dreams
of One East Africa

They called themselves the Happiness Club and for me, a Kenyan, returning to the region of my birth for the first time since I fled into exile from the dictatorial regime of Daniel Toroitich arap Moi in June 1982, they symbolised the essential East Africa. It was April 1987, I had just arrived in Dar es Salaam from London via Harare, a guest of Walter Bgoya, and here I was in the midst of a group dedicated to Happiness. Only two months before, February, the Kenya police had siezed my novel, *Matigari,* and I was wondering what they would do to the author if they knew that he was now just across the border with the Happiness Club. The members and their guests were not all Muslims; but they had gathered for dinner in the house of a Tanzanian woman of Asian origin to celebrate the end of the fast of Ramadhani. She wore a long kanga cloth and she spoke flawless Kiswahili. My eyes kept on moving from her to another woman, a Tanzanian of Arab-African origin, whose ebony neck and face were casually but beautifully profiled by a white satin cloth which fell in folds over her shoulders. She was born in Zanzibar, and now lived in Dar es Salaam. The men were mostly from Tanzania, Uganda, Somalia and I from Kenya. Two of the men wore long white kanzus and Muslim caps; the rest wore Western clothes.

The dinner was a feast of fish, lamb, chicken in curried coconut gravy, chapatis, parathas, spinach, pawpaws, and other varieties of tropical greens and fruits. And of course rice. From another room where the younger people were, there drifted Tarabu music with its hints of Arabia, India, Africa and even Cuba blended into one. I savoured the smell of the food; the music of the voices; the colours of the clothes; the anecdotes and the stories; the warmth of the laughter of the evening, for all these, even the feast of Ramadhani bespoke the East Africa of my upbringing and experience.

I was born in 1938 in Limuru, Kenya, near Kamīrīīthū, where then stood what we called the 'Swahili' village but which really was simply a Muslim settlement. Their style of dressing – earrings, noserings, black buibuis, ntandios, colourful kangas, embroidered caps – and their tinroofed houses were very much the same as I was later to see in Mombasa and Nakuru, Kenya; in Kampala, Uganda; and in Dar es Salaam, Tanzania. It was as if the coast had been reproduced in the different parts of East Africa. As a child I played with others in Kamīrīīthū who bore names like Juma, Abdi, Omali, Amina besides others who answered to names like John, Peter, Samuel, and Margaret; and of course the majority who had the more common African names like Kamau, Onyango, Mulwa and Akinyi.

We always envied the dwellers of the Muslim village when Ramadhani ended. They always ate plenty of white gleaming rice, something we had only at Christmas, but even then in small quantities. Thus Christmas and Ramadhani were oddly connected in my mind, with rice and chapatis being the real material symbolic links. It was years, many years later, that I realised that chapatis, parathas and curries were of Indian origin and were also used in Hindu festivals like the Diwali, the festival of light, which the Indian kids in Limuru town used to celebrate with fireworks. Christmas, Ramadhani, Diwali, the Irua initiation ceremony among the Agīkūyū: all these were connected together by curry and rice. That was in the fifties.

In 1978 Ramadhani and Kamīrīīthū were to reappear in my life. I was then in political detention-without-trial at Kamītī maximum security prison in Kenya because of my activities in community theatre at Kamīrīīthū, and more so because of writing plays in a language, an African language, that people of the area could understand. The Muslim village had long disappeared, actually destroyed by the colonial administration in the fifties during the Mau Mau-led armed struggle. But in my cell at Kamītī, I one day recalled it because it was a Ramadhani festival that interrupted our monotonous rhythm of the filthy prison food that passed for a diet. Some of the political prisoners were Muslims and they were given special permission to have rice, white gleaming rice, at the end of the feast. We all took part in the eating.

Now, here in Dar es Salaam, I was marking my temporary return to the region with a Ramadhani feast in the company of Muslims, Christians and others who were neither of these but who were all members or guests of the Happiness Club. This was East Africa. A kalaidoscope of colours, cultures, and contours of history.

After the feast we went to the Indian Ocean to cap the evening's Happiness with fishing at midnight in a motorboat belonging to the lady in white satin. We headed for Mbudya and other tiny islands. The moon and the stars were reflected in the slightly moving folds of the surface of the sea. As the land gradually receded behind us I began to understand why Dar es Salaam had been named so: the Haven of Peace. The roaring of the engine or even our voices raised in fishermen's songs or anecdotes, only deepened the encircling peace. The silence was pregnant with memories.

In the days when there were no steamships, the monsoon winds provided the sailing power which enabled seasonal migrations between this East African coast and all the others bordering the Red Sea and the Indian Ocean, particularly those of Arabia, Persia, India and Ceylon. From May to September the ships went away with the south-westerly winds; but from November to March, the north-easterly winds reversed the process. The ensuing trade turned East Africa into a prosperous area, the subject matter of poetic imagination and travellers' tales. Between the tenth and fifteenth centuries, with the incorporation of the area into the worldwide Muslim culture and commerce extending from the coast to the Sahara, West Africa and Spain, there arose several city states with Islam as part of the way of life and Kiswahili as the unifying language of culture and commerce. Preeminent among them were Kilwa, Mombasa, and Malindi, celebrated in Milton's *Paradise Lost* as among the cities and civilisations which Angel Gabriel showed Adam and Eve as visions of the future just before their expulsion from Paradise. They were a kind of paradise regained through human efforts aided by the monsoon winds.

On the night of Happiness we were therefore fishing in the waterways of history, waters which had seen the rise and fall of these peculiarly East African cities whose cosmopolitan culture was so well reflected in the food, the clothes, the music and even the composition of the Happiness Club.

The boat stopped at different places and we would cast our lines and baits into the waters. The silence of the sea was now so profound that we were all drawn into it and the conversation was reduced to the level of whisperings. If we went southwards from here, my host is explaining to me, we would end up in Kilwa. We go straight across, and we end up in Zanzibar and Pemba. But northwards we come to Bagamoyo and even beyond to Mombasa and Malindi. You would then be back home in Kenya. Well, I feel at home already . . . I tell him. You are right . . . East Africa is really one country.

A line drawing of a map of the physical features of Kenya, Uganda and Tanzania looks to me like a sketch of a bust of a human head wearing a slightly flat muslim cap whose slightly flattened top is the long border with Ethiopia. The neck rests on the Ruvuma river to the south. The back is formed by the tiny folds of the coastline on the Indian Ocean. The face is the line of lakes to the west from Malawi to Albert with Lake Tanganyika and Kivu making the outline of the chin and mouth. Lakes Edward and Albert form a retreating forehead. This strong human shaped head is facing into the heart and belly of the continent.

Indeed the rivers form a network of waterways linking East Africa to the continent and they contribute to the oceans that link East Africa to the world. Tana river with its origin in snow-capped Mount Kenya; Athi river with its origin in the Ngong hills and Mount Kilimanjaro; Pangani from Kilimanjaro and Meru; the Rufiji river; all flow into the Indian Ocean. Other streams and rivers from Lake Tanganyika join the mighty Congo into the Atlantic Ocean. The Nile, the most famous of them all, originates from Lake Victoria, through Kioga and Albert, into the Mediterranean Sea. Lake Victoria itself is fed by numerous rivers with sources in the highlands of Kenya, Uganda and Tanzania. Lake Victoria is truly Lake East Africa and it should be renamed so.

Then there are the famous mountains: Ruwenzori, Elgon, Kenya, Kilimanjaro. They are very East African with Kilimanjaro shared by both Kenya and Tanzania and Elgon by Kenya and Uganda. Standing tall into the sky, they are the natural guardians of our land, really the permanent seat of God watching over Africa. Kilimanjaro after all is the highest in the Continent. The Ruwenzoris are the legendary Mountains of the Moon; and Kenya and Kilimanjaro excited nineteenth-century Europe with the reports of their having defied the equatorial sun by wearing permanent caps of snow.

The Great Rift Valley is another natural feature that is uniquely East Africa. From Beira to Mozambique, it forks into a V-shape at the north end of Lake Malawi. The western half of the V contains the necklace of lakes that make the western boundary from Tanzania to Uganda; while the eastern half, containing the lakes from Eyasi and Manyara to Turkana, goes through the heartlands of Tanzania and Kenya all the way to the Red Sea and beyond.

This landscape of mountains, lakes, rivers, hills, great valleys and a coastline endowed with natural harbours has affected East African history profoundly. For years the coast had connected East Africa to the world, to as far as China where giraffes had already reached, the gifts of the King of Malindi to the Chinese Emperors. The good, the bad and even the ugly had come from the sea, the ugliest being the Portuguese presence at the end of the fifteenth century that ushered in the more than four hundred years of unequal relationship with Western Europe. In the wars of resistance against foreign occupation the mountains formed a natural fortress to which our forces retreated for refuge and sustenance and as rear bases. And of course the richness of the earth became the central bone of contention between Europe and East Africa in the twentieth century. Not surprisingly the natural landscape dominates the East African literary imagination. This awareness of the land as the central actor in our lives distinguishes East African literature from others in the continent and it certainly looms large in my own writings from *The River Between* to *Matigari*.

Limuru, where I was born, is on the edge of the Rift Valley. The escarpment and the forest bush around it were part of my growing up and I have never stopped being overwhelmed by the sight of the valley from the Limuru end. It becomes even more mysterious when it is covered by the mist in the morning or evening.

The railway line built by the British in 1901 to connect Kenya to Uganda descends into the mighty Rift at a point not very far from my childhood home. We used to stand on a hill and watch the trains bound for Uganda steaming away and it seemed to us that they were actually singing about their journey. We made up a song to the rhythm of the movement of the trains:

Nda-thiĩ-ū-ganda
Nda-thiĩ-ū-ganda

I-am-go-ing-to-u-ganda
I-am-go-ing-to-u-ganda

We would quicken the pace of the song to keep up with the speed-ing of the train to a climax when the train seemed to be saying nothing more than just the repetition of the word Uganda. Uganda then seemed far far away and really it would have been nice if the train could have carried us there.

Later in 1959 the train did carry me to Uganda, to Kampala, and on to Makerere University College, then an external wing of the University of London, where I read English literature and where I was to discover myself as a writer.

Kampala is a city of high hills. Makerere, after which the college was named, is one of the nine hills on which the city stands. But the name Makerere had come to symbolise higher learning in East Africa and for those who ascended the hill it meant a passage into the membership of a band of the very elect. But the college was more than that.

In the fifties and early sixties Makerere was the intellectual capital of East and Central Africa, a role later taken over by the Dar es Salaam University of the early sixties. The majority of the students came from Kenya, Uganda and Tanzania. Tanzania was then in its two separate identities of Tanganyika and Zanzibar. But there were others from Malawi (then Nyasaland), Zambia (then Northern Rhodesia), and Zimbabwe (then Southern Rhodesia). As students, members of the same institution, we became accustomed to doing things together. An example of this was the running of the students clubs and associations and particularly the main students body, Makerere Students Guild. These were led by whoever commanded the confidence of the majority no matter the country of their ori-gins. We were East Africans, Pan-Africanists, at least we regarded ourselves as such, and we were proud of it.

For us Kenyans, Uganda of the fifties held a special significance and fascination. All my life I had been surrounded by a white colonial settler presence. Kenya like Uganda had become a British sphere of influence with the carving up of the continent at the

164

infamous Berlin Conference in 1884. But unlike Uganda, Kenya was targeted for white settlement. With the building of the Kenya – Uganda railway, the settlers came and kept on coming, and they were determined to make Kenya a whiteman's country. Born just before the outbreak of the Second World War, growing up in Limuru I assumed that the white presence, owners of the tea plantations and mansions across the railway, were a normal part of our lives. This normality was challenged by the Mau Mau in 1952. The settler presence reacted to the challenge with white terror. Kenya came under a State of Emergency. Through this, the British colonial regime had hoped to contain the Mau Mau resistance and the Kenya people's fight for independence. In practice this meant terrorising the entire African population. Thus going into Uganda during that period was an escape from the terror that stalked our daily lives. An escape? There was also a sense of arrival, a sense of homecoming. Except for a comparatively small Indian presence in Kampala and other urban centres, Uganda was visibly, clearly, unarguably an African people's country. Before this, I had never had the experience of being and living in a country of blacks without whites.

It was Makerere and Uganda which made me discover my sense of being a Kenyan. It had established a home, a base, and a distance from which I could look back on my Kenyan experience and try to recapture its meaning in words. There were literary journals like *Penpoint* and later *Transition* to take in some of my earliest attempts in that direction. *The Black Hermit*, a play; the two novels, *The River Between* and *Weep Not, Child*; numerous short stories and journalism were written while I was a student at Makerere. It was also at Makerere that we celebrated the very first Independence in East, Central and Southern Africa – the Independence of Tanganyika, later Tanzania, in 1961 – which was also a celebration of a new dawn in the region.

Tanzania came to occupy a very special place in the political imagination of East Africans. It was not simply because of her history of anti-colonial resistance, symbolised by the great Maji Maji armed struggle in 1905 and independence in 1961. It was not even because of her later role in the liberation of Southern Africa although this has been a great contribution at great national self-sacrifice. In the sixties and early seventies Tanzania provided an anti-neo-colonial intellectual and political leadership best

165

symbolised by the University of Dar es Salaam becoming the intellectual revolutionary hub of East Africa, Africa, and the Third World generally. In its heydey Dar es Salaam attracted a brilliant crowd of progressive scholars from all over the world, Africa in particular, whose thought and actions are still influencing the shape of things in East Africa. Walter Rodney's *How Europe Underdeveloped Africa*; Issa Shivji's *The Silent Class Struggle*; *The Dar Debate on Imperialism, Nationality and Class* – these and more produced by academics who had been at the Dar Campus and all published by Tanzania Publishing House in its days of glory under Walter Bgoya, have become part of the common intellectual heritage of East Africa. Julius Nyerere became the philosopher-king some of whose words still fire my own thinking on education and culture. The new education in the post-colonial era was for self-reliance economically, politically, culturally and psychologically. Otherwise as he once told teachers at Dar es Salaam,

> You will teach to produce clerks as the colonialists did. You will not be teaching fighters but a bunch of slaves and semi-slaves. Get your pupils out of the colonial mentality. You have to produce tough people; stubborn youths – who can do something – not hopeless youths.

Julius Nyerere was a student at Makerere when it was the intellectual capital of East Africa. The present day Ugandan leader, Yoweri Museveni, was a student at Dar es Salaam University when it was the revolutionary mecca of East Africa.

Under Nyerere, Tanzania was also behind two declarations, first Nairobi and later Arusha, which are still part of the political agenda in East Africa because they address themselves to the themes of unity and social change. They held aloft the banner of hope, visions of tomorrow to which we all could relate, because they seemed such a clear and logical outcome of what was happening in the region. What a time it was, those days at Makerere, in East Africa! It was a replica of the Wordsworthian bliss at being alive at the birth of a revolution and the possibilities of a new future. Africa, Our Africa, was coming back.

They had been meeting in Nairobi for a few days and then on 5 June

1963 they announced their pledge to merge the three countries into
a political Union. What! An East African Federation? Tanganyika,
with Julius Nyerere as the first Prime Minister and later President,
had been independent for over a year; Uganda, under Apollo
Milton Obote as the Premier, for slightly over six months; and
Kenya had just attained internal self rule with Jomo Kenyatta,
recently released from eight years in prison as a Mau Mau convict, as
its Prime Minister. Yet their declaration for a larger political unit
had no hesitation and no ambiguities:

> Our meeting, they said, is motivated by the spirit of Pan-Afri-
> canism and not by mere selfish regional interest . . . There is no
> more room for slogans and words. This is our day of action in the
> cause of the ideals we believe in, and in the unity and freedom for
> which we have suffered and sacrificed so much.

It was not the first time that the federation of the three territories
had been discussed. From 1919, or since Tanganyika was taken over
from the Germans, the British Government had tried to bring about
a closer union of the three colonies. The various efforts resulted in
some services like transport and customs being run on an East African basis from about 1932. The Governors of the three countries
began regular meetings, with Kenya in the chair. In 1948 the Governors conference was replaced by a High Commission as the execu-
tive arm, and an East Africa Assembly as the legislative arm. In
1961, the High Commission changed its name and status and it now
became East Africa Common Services Organisation with a 'Parliament' – The Central Legislative Assembly.

What had escaped all the previous efforts was the formal act of
political union. In colonial times the people most keen on such a
union with a central state were the white settlers in Kenya. They
could see their economic hold on the region being strengthened by
their control of such a state. The African people had always opposed
it for the same reasons. But now, with independence promising a
new era of paramountcy of African interests, a centralised East African state could only strengthen them. Our time had come!

The declaration was met with ululations by the people of the
three countries. In the villages, in the towns, in the streets, everywhere, the workers, peasants and the youth composed songs in
support of it:

Tulimtuma Nyerere
Kwa Uhuru
Kenya, Uganda, Tanganyika
Sisi twasaidiana

We sent Nyerere
On a mission for freedom
Kenya, Uganda, Tanganyika
We support one another

I was then a student at Makerere and I can remember the excitement at the news. After all, we the students had been doing things together as East Africans. Our unity was now about to flower and bear a big and juicy political fruit in the very creation of an East African federation promised with so much fanfare at the end of 1963.

We had a chance to express our feelings. One day we heard that the three leaders, Nyerere, Obote and Kenyatta, were going to have a public meeting at the Clock Tower in Kampala. It was a Saturday, the 29th of June, 1963. We trooped to the meeting ground singing and dancing: Uhuru cha cha cha . . . Umoja cha cha cha . . . The meeting was well attended and our student voices joined those of the working people who had massed there. Thunderous applause greeted Nyerere, or Obote or Kenyatta when any of them referred to their Nairobi declaration. Uhuru cha cha cha . . . Unity cha cha cha . . .

What were we really cheering? The three leaders could tabulate all the advantages of an East African federation. These were obvious and even the white settlers had correctly identified them in earlier years. Western interests would not have opposed such a closer unity, particularly if it ensured a greater and more secure territory for their operations. But the fact is that the Nairobi declaration had not really addressed itself to the ideology guiding the foundation of such a federation. Whose state was it going to be? What social interests in East Africa was it going to serve? Where did it stand *vis-à-vis* neo-colonialism and the fundamental question of social change for the majority, the working people of East Africa so well represented by the crowd that had gathered at the Clock Tower?

And then came the Arusha declaration, addressing itself to Tanzania only. But in some ways it was more East African than the

Nairobi declaration. Arusha reflected realities and articulated a vision beyond the borders of Tanzania:

> We have been oppressed a great deal, we have been exploited a great deal and we have been degraded a great deal. It is our weakness that has led to our being oppressed, exploited, disregarded. Now we want a revolution – a revolution which brings to an end our weakness so that we are never again exploited, oppressed and humiliated.

With the Arusha declaration, Nyerere and Tanzania had secured their place in the political imagination of East Africa for years to come, for in articulating the vision of the emancipation of the workers and peasants of Tanzania, they were actually stating the links that really bound the peoples of the three territories. The fact is that the working people of all three areas had been exploited a great deal, oppressed a great deal, humiliated a great deal and only the unity and the economic, political and cultural empowerment of the masses would meet the real needs.

As it turned out, the Nairobi declaration and the Clock Tower meeting at Kampala were to remain the pinnacle of the dreams for a centralised East African state. The Arusha declaration was to bring out sharply and clearly the different paths of social development opted for by the three states. Tanzania was experimenting with social democracy, under the name Ujamaa. Kenya grew into a classical neo-colony, preferring its cosy relationship with the West, as client state, to the risks of a different social order. The Kenya leadership took it that it was better to be a well-fed slave than to chance the search for self reliance as a free and independent nation. Uganda under Obote tried to face different directions at the same time, signalling right, left and centre simultaneously. And then with the *coup d'état* of Idi Amin, fascism came to Uganda. In the end, even the East African Community which had replaced the East African Common Services Organisation could not be saved. In 1978 Tanzania and Uganda went to war. The border between Kenya and Tanzania was closed between 1977 and 1983. And since the fall of Idi Amin and of the second reign of Obote, Dictator Moi has tried his best to provoke a war with Museveni's Uganda. Thus today in the nineties, the three countries seem no nearer a political union than they were in 1963 when Nyerere, Obote and Kenyatta made the Nairobi declaration and thrilled the hearts of millions. Does it mean that the declaration was only sound and fury signifying nothing?

East Africa is condemned by the inheritance of geography and history to forever keep on trying to forge unity for its common survival as a strong force in Africa and world affairs or else be doomed to remain weak, subject to humiliations and manipulations by other more powerful nations. Our history has already given us a number of legacies, as guides and warnings, on which we can forge real unity. Two of the most crucial are the gifts of a common language and a common tradition of resistance to foreign domination and struggle against internal repression.

An overwhelming number of scholars now accept that Kiswahili is an African language. It is originally the language of the Waswahili at the coast and it clearly belongs to the Bantu group of languages. But it has been enriched by cultural contact with the different forces which have interacted with East Africa. Its capacity to absorb new words, new expressions, new experiences, makes it .one of the fastest-growing languages in the world. It is today the national and official language in Tanzania; it is the all-Kenya national language, despite the fact that English is still the official language; and it is assuming a similar position in Uganda. We have many languages in East Africa. But Kiswahili enables us to communicate across all the different languages. The beauty of it is that this is an African language, an authentic product of East Africa, of our history, and in its development at the coast, it always functioned as a language of unity, facilitating culture contact and commerce.

Resistance is yet another common theme in our history. By the fifteenth century at the coast and up to the eighteenth century in the interior, the struggles with nature itself as well as social struggles through trade, commerce, and even inter-community wars, were bringing about the integration of the various regions into ever larger units and formations often with .a centralised authority, the Bunyoro-Kitara, Ankole and Buganda kingdoms in Uganda, and the Ntemi chiefdoms in Tanzania, being the best examples. The process of the internal workings-out of the contradictions with nature; of contradictions between communities; and contradictions within a community was interrupted by the various invaders from the sea. The Portuguese in the sixteenth and seventeenth centuries were followed by those of the Omanite Arabs of the eighteenth century; and then those of the Germans and the British in nineteenth century. Divide and rule was the common theme in the practice of these conquerors. Division of the East African communities by external forces is best symbolised by the Berlin Conference of 1884 which, with the subsequent treaties, saw the various boundaries drawn literally through even single language communities so that today the three territories share certain nationalities who live on either side of their borders. The Maasai, for instance, inhabit both Tanzania and Kenya. It is the struggle against these external forces of occupation that created the common tradition of resistance.

Kenya provides one of the best examples of this tradition. I need hardly mention all the wars fought by the Mombasans against the Portuguese in the last years of the fifteenth century and throughout the sixteenth, and the seventeenth centuries. One of the most memorable was the 1630 resistance led by Yusuf bin Hasan against the Portuguese occupation of Mombasa. Another memorable event was the three-year siege of Mombasa towards the end of the seventeenth century, which finally broke the backbone of the Portuguese presence at the East African coast. By 1728 the Portuguese had been driven out of Kenya never to return, leaving behind Fort Jesus, destroyed cities, and a few words as the only mark of their two hundred years presence. Similar feats of resistance were later enacted against the Omanites, the Germans, and the British, in the three countries. The Maji Maji armed struggle against the Germans in Tanzania in 1905 began the era of armed anti-colonial uprisings. It was however the Mau Mau armed struggle from 1952 to 1962 which captured the imagination of all East Africa and which best symbolised the determination of the African people to be free. And just as the three-year siege of Mombasa in the seventeenth century broke the back of the Portuguese occupation, so did the Mau Mau break the back of the entire British colonial policy in East Africa and beyond. Colonial control could no longer be effected in the old way. From the Great Mombasa resistance through Maji Maji to Mau Mau, our history glitters with many heroic characters: Yusuf bin Hasan, Mbarak Ibn Rashid, Mwakawa, Kabarega, Mwanga, and Kĩmathi: all these honour that great tradition of resistance.

There are other lessons from that history. Those at the forefront in the struggle against foreign occupation and domination were the forces most conscious of the need for unity within the various national communities. Such a leadership always felt it necessary to draw closer to the people, getting their strength from the broad masses. Those that allied with foreign occupation and domination always worked against the unity of the various peoples. Collaboration with the foreign invader always alienated such individuals and leaders from the people. They therefore ruled through tyranny. Or putting it another way, tyrannies always thrived through divisions among the peoples and between communities.

Still the people had an answer to tyranny. In his book *The Meadows of Gold and the Mines of Gems* written in Cairo in 943 AD, al Mas'udi, who had travelled to the East Africa coast in 916 AD, describes the people as being ruled by a supreme king under whom were other smaller kings. Such kings were chosen on the condition that they ruled in justice:

> Once the king becomes a tyrant, and stops ruling justly they kill him and refuse to allow his descendants to inherit the throne. They do this because in ceasing to rule justly the king has ceased to be the son of the Supreme Lord that is to say the God of Heaven and Earth.

Thus our history of resistance is full of guides and warnings about our present and our future. So simple and yet so easy to forget. In unity lies strength; in divisions, weakness.

With the inheritance of a common geography, a common tradition of resistance, a common language, and with political unity bringing about the economic integration of our 60 million people under one strong federal state, what a wonderful base this would be from which we could face the twenty-first century. This substantial home market would enable us to sustain big modern industries, raise our agricultural production to new heights, open up internal tourism, develop complementary economic activities instead of the current duplication, and exploit all the possibilities of internal commerce long before we need explore foreign markets. We could interact with foreign markets on the basis of strength, not weakness, equality and not dependence. We would in the process say farewell to colonial borders and the divisions of nationalities as we leap into the twenty-first century. A midnight dream of an amateur fisherman on the high seas? The dream was not mine alone: It has been with us on the land and on the sea.

'Tanzania, Uganda and Kenya once had a dream – or a vision – that we would all become part of one large unit. Some of us still hold on to that dream, and believe it can be made into a reality,' so said Julius Nyerere on 7 June 1968, probably referring to the Nairobi declaration which had promised to bring about a federation at the end of 1963.

Today the architects of the Nairobi declaration are no longer on the scene. Kenyatta is dead, Obote out of power. Nyerere is no longer the head of state. And while Tanzania under Mwinyi, and Uganda, under Museveni, are still experimenting with forms of democratic participation in the national life and have adopted a pro-Africa policy in international relations, Kenya, under Moi, has become a dictatorship crushing any forms of popular participation in the political and cultural life of the country. The Moi/Kanu regime has given military facilities to the USA; and under the guise of merely providing tropical conditions for their training, the regime has ensured a British military presence in the country. The country has become a tourist paradise for Western hunters of sex, sun and sand. Malindi for instance is now German territory. Other areas of the coast have been colonised by American, Italian, and British tourists. The dictatorship with its vast machinery of terror – more than five people cannot meet even for a family tea party, funeral or wedding without a police licence – was in the era of the Cold War never exposed in the West because of its alignment. Hundreds of political prisoners rot in Moi's jails. Others are in exile. The gap between the rich and the poor is one of the widest in Africa. The dictatorship has set nationalities and regions against one another. If it is so scared of democracy and unity within Kenya, how could it possibly welcome democracy and unity on a far larger scale?

But the dream and the vision are still there among the progressive youth of the three countries. For instance the 1987 Draft Minimum Programme of Mwakenya – the underground resistance movement in Kenya – states as one of its goals the realisation of the political unity of the three East African countries 'on the basis of the indivisible common interests of the peasants and workers' and 'on the firm conviction that many of our problems can be solved more effectively on an East African basis.'

What emerges is that genuine African unity on a continental or regional basis will not be possible unless founded on consistent anti-neo-colonialism and democracy. Such unity would have to be sought from the standpoint of the people. It cannot be imposed from above or from without. A commitment to genuine independence, democracy and social change is essential to the success of any new phase in the struggle for regional and even continental economic, political and cultural integration. For that reason I prefer the poetry of the Arusha declaration to the inflated prose of the Nairobi declaration. For only on the basis of profound social change, an increase in wealth and the insurance that the wealth remains within the country and within the majority, can there be genuine social justice and happiness for all in any one of the countries or in one East Africa.

Since my exile in 1982, I have been a wanderer. I have lived and worked in many places, my latest being as Visiting Professor at Yale University in the USA. But there is a Kenya I always carry with me, a Kenya that nobody, not even Dictator Moi, can take from me. It is the Kenya of the working people of all the nationalities within it and their heroic struggles against domination by nature or other humans, over the centuries. In my novels, I have tried to capture this sense of national pride and dignity. It is the working people of Kenya who took on the post-war might of the British Empire and forced colonialism to retreat for fear that Mau Mau-type armed insurrections might break out in other parts of the British-colonised world. But the neo-colonial state under Moi has been at war with this aspect of our history. The facts testify to this.

When in 1977 I co-authored, with Ngũgĩ wa Mĩriĩ, a play, *Ngaahika Ndeenda*, celebrating the fact that the ordinary people, and not outstanding individuals, are the makers of our history, I was arrested and placed in a maximum security prison. How dare I write that about people and in a language that those very people could understand? When in 1982, we tried to perform another play, *Maitũ Njugĩra*, again celebrating the same kind of history, the police closed the theatre where we were due to perform and later

Moi sent three truckloads of armed policemen to raze to the ground the Kamīrīīthū open air theatre. And lastly when later I wrote a novel, *Matigari*, on the same theme, and it was published in Gīkūyū in Kenya in 1986, the results were even more dramatic.

Matigari, the main character, is puzzled by a world where the producer is not the one who has the last word on what he has produced; a world where lies are rewarded and truth punished. He goes round the country asking questions about truth and justice. People who had read the novel started talking about Matigari and the questions he was raising as if Matigari was a real person in life. When Dictator Moi heard that there was a Kenyan roaming around the country asking such questions, he issued orders for the man's arrest. But when the police found that he was only a character in fiction, Moi was even more angry and he issued fresh orders for the arrest of the book itself. That's why, in February 1987, in a very well co-ordinated police action, the novel was seized from all the bookshops and from the publisher's warehouse. The novel is now published in English for a readership outside Kenya, the first case, in our history, of a fictional character being forced into exile to join its creator. But this was Moi's Kenya where facts are stranger than fiction, where state actions in the streets here induced more terror in its citizens than that of their nightmares, where the words of the head of state about himself, spoken in all seriousness, would more than match those of the cleverest of satirists.

I am telling my host about Matigari's Africa as we return to the mainland from our midnight fishing in the Indian Ocean. The story has emerged from the current joke in the boat: that he and I belong more to the world of publishing than to that of fishing. The ocean had been mean with us, yielding us only two tiny fishes after three hours of throwing hook, line and sinker into its waters. He is suggesting turning the book into a film so that Matigari would return to East Africa as a visual image. Strange that we too are talking about Matigari as if he was indeed a real person. But on or out of celluloid, I know, in a sense more deep than words can tell, that Matigari shall one day return to Kenya, to East Africa, for his world is shared by the essential East Africa once envisioned in the Arusha declaration and the glimpses of which we still get when looking at our history as East Africans.

As later in the week I board Air Tanzania for Harare I cannot help thinking that this was once part of the mighty East African Airways, senselessly wrecked in the seventies because Moi and his then close associates wanted to start a private airline. I recall the Happiness Club who had given me a little happiness to carry back with me on the highways of the world. And despite the fact that I was literally next to Kenya and I, like Matigari, could not set foot on the land of my birth, I was happy. For I had been in touch with East Africa, my East Africa, communing for a time with the dreams and visions of a politically united region as a prelude to the United States of Africa. Africa will come back!

Index

Abdulla, Abdulatif, 45, 94, 104; *Kenya, Where Are We Heading to?*, 94; *The Voice of Agony*, 94
Abrahams, Peter, 105–6, 150; *Tell Freedom*, 4, 61
Achebe, Chinua, 7, 13 *Things Fall Apart*, 61; *A Man of the People*, 67
Achimota University, Ghana, 106
Adagala, Seth, 92
Aeschylus, 13
Africa: in European fiction, 133
African bourgeoisie, 63, 64–5, 84–5; Petty-bourgeois inherited management of ex-colonies, 51–2
African centres of progressive thought, 70
African countries, from colonies to neo-colonies, 48–9, 69; armed struggles and *coups d'état*, 69
African culture, imperialist-sanctioned and patriotic national, 44
African languages: growth of writing in, xiv; revitalised, 23–4; never met English as equals, 35; used by African writers, 20–1
African literature, 20; the politics of language in, 10
African National Congress, South Africa, 79, 150
African novels: titles indicative of alienation, 107–8
African writers: emergence after Second World War, 112; set aside by education and language choice, 107; using African languages, 20–1; writing in European languages, 84
Afro-European literature, 8–9, 19–20
Algeria, 99, 100, 149

All-Africa Conference of Churches, 93
Alliance High School, Kenya, 136–8
Amin, Idi, 67, 105
Amin, Samir, 70; *Eurocentrism*, xvi
Andersen, Hans Christian, 13
Angola, 64, 69, 78–9, 99, 100
Anti-colonial struggles for independence, 17, 60, 69, 73, 111
Apartheid, South Africa, 60, 81, 110, 120–1, 149
Arabic, 35
Aramaic, 33n
Archimedes, 33
Armah, Ayi Kwei: *The Beautyful Ones Are Not Yet Born*, 67, 108
Arusha declaration on unity of East Africa, 166, 169, 174–5
Awoonor, Kofi, 104

Baker, Kenneth, former Education Secretary, UK government, 33–4, 36, 38
Bakhtin: *From the Prehistory of Novelistic Discourse*, 22
Baldwin, James, 7
Balzac, Honoré de, 38; *Eugénie Grandet*, 132
Berlin conference (1884), 47, 88, 110, 164, 171; Africa carved up into spheres of influence, 37
Bgoya, Walter, 159, 166
Biggles, 136–141
Black Writers' Congresses, 113
Blake, William, 14, 25, 38
Blixen, Karen, alias Isaak Dinesen, xiii, 35, 133–5; *Out of Africa*, xiii, 35; *Shadows on the Grass*, xiii, 134

179

Index

Bokassa, Jean Bédel, 67
Brazil, 119
Brecht, Bertolt, 13, 38, 105
Britain, 36, 143
British colonialism, 60, 143; in Kenya,
  88–9
British Empire, The, 143
Bromley, D. Alan, US national advisor in
  sciences and technology, 154
Brutus, Dennis, 104
Buchan, John, 140
Burkina Faso, (formerly Upper Volta):
  Sankara's coup, 69
Bush, George, President of USA, 154

Cabral, Amilcar, 70
Cameroon, 155
capitalism: the fight with labour, 118–121
Caribbean literature: author's research on,
  7
Carlyle, Thomas, 123
Cary, Joyce, 4
Cervantes, Miguel de, 22
Césaire, Aimé, 7; Return to My Native
  Land, 10
Chaucer, Geoffrey, 6
Chile, 119; Allende regime overthrown,
  68; under Pinochet, 51
China, 112
Chinese language, 35, 40
Chinweizu: The West and the Rest of Us,
  28
Chowdhury, Kashim: Our City, 144
Clark, J.P.: Ozidi Saga, 18
Coetzee, David, 20; Foe, 17
collaborationist Africans, 63, 130; in
  Kenya, 97
collaborationist literature, 18
Collins, Brian: 'Our Country Now', 142
colonialism, 16–7, 42–3, 60, 111, 123,
  143; destroying languages, history, 42;
  indirect rule, 32; in Kenya, 88–9;
  movements for independence from, 64,
  111, 149–150, 165; violence on
  colonised communities, 28
Congo (Brazzaville), 64
Conrad, Joseph, 4, 5–6, 38; Lord Jim, 5;
  Victory, 5, 6; Nostromo, 5, 6; Heart of
  Darkness, 5, 6, 16
coups d'état in African countries, 66, 69
Cuba, 112
Cuffy, William, 145
Cugoano, Ottobah, 145

culture: as carrier of a people's moral,
  aesthetic and ethical values, 27; best
  measure of humanity, 56; product of a
  people's history, 42

Danish Library Association, 133, 135
Dar es Salaam University, 8, 165, 166;
  Debate on Class, State and Imperialism,
  70
Davidson, William, 145
Defoe, Daniel: Robinson Crusoe, 15, 17
De Klerk, F.W., 146
Development Assistance for the Nineties,
  workshop, Stockholm, 154
Dickens, Charles, 38, 136; Oliver Twist,
  136–7
Diop, Cheikh Anita, 21
Diop, David, 21; poem Africa, 61–2
Dostoevsky, Fyodor, 13
DuBois, W.E.B., 129, 148, 150

East Africa, 155; 'really one country',
  162; early British efforts at federation,
  167
East African Federation pledge (1963),
  167; as prelude to United States of
  Africa, 176
Eliot, George: Middlemarch, 10
Eliot, T.S., 6
Ellison, Ralph, 7
El Salvador, 51, 119
EMERGE, African-American news
  magazine, xiii
English language, 8, 11, 26, 32–3, 34,
  35, 37, 40–1, 170; arrival in Third
  World, 31; English: A Language for the
  World?, BBC seminar (1988), 30;
  language of African literature, 107;
  never met African languages as equals,
  35; racist tradition, 38; relationship to
  various languages of world, 30
Equiano, Olaudah, 145; The Interesting
  Life of Olaudah Equiano, or Gustavus
  Vassa, The African, 104
Eurocentrism, xvi; or Afrocentrism, 8–9
European literature, 18; humanistic side,
  14
Evening Standard newspaper, London, 33,
  36

Fanon, Frantz, 10, 120; The Wretched of
  the Earth (Les Damnés de la Terre), 2,
  3, 65, 66, and chapter 'The Pitfalls of
  National Consciousness', 3, 66

Faulkner, William, 13
FESTAC, 13
FLN, Algeria: struggles against French colonialism, 60, 69
Franco, General, 123
French language, 8, 11, 32, 35, 37, 40–1; arrival in Third World, 31; as language of new African literature, 107
Froude, James, 123
Fryer, Peter: *Staying Power: The History of Black People in Britain*, 142, 145

Gakaara wa Wanjaū, 89–90, 104
Gama, Vasco da, 148
Gandhi, Mahatma, 150
Gecau, Kīmani, 45, 72, 105
Geertz, Professor, 25, 26, 27; *Local Knowledge: Fact and Law in Comparative Perspective*, 25
German language, 40
Ghana, 61, 66; independence (1957), 60; Rawlings' coup, 69
Gīkūyū, xiii, 90, 94, 155, 156; author's decision to write in, 9; taught at Yale University, 156
Goethe, Johann Wolfgang von, 13, 22
Gogol, Nicolai, 22
Goody, Jack, Professor, 25
Graft, Joe de: *Muntu*, 93
Greek language, 33n
Greene, Graham, 38
Grimm Brothers, 13
griot tradition of West African oral histories, 19
Guinea-Bissau, 64, 69, 99, 100
Guma, Alex la, 13, 38, 104, 150
Gurr, Andrew, Professor, 9, 102; *Writers in Exile*, 107

Happiness Club, The, 159–161, 176
Hasan, Yusuf bin, 171
Hausa language, 38, 156
Hebrew language, 38, 33n
Hegel, Friedrich, xiv, 123, 130
Hemingway, Ernest, 105
Hetata, Sherif, 104
Hitler, Adolph, 123
Ho Chi Min, 147
Hola Camp, Kenya, 149
Hume, David, 123, 130
Hutchinson, Alfred, 61; *Road to Ghana*, 61
Huxley, Elspeth, 35; *Flame Trees of Thika*, 45

Ibadan University, Nigeria, 106
Iliad, The, 22
imperialism, 45, 47, 83; conquest of labour power, 42; cultural tradition, 43; enemy of mankind, 73; not able to destroy fighting culture, 45; peace impossible in world dominated by, 125; power of dead capital, 110; three centres of in 1990s, 53
independence movements, 64, 111, 149–150, 165
International Book Fair of Radical, Black and Third World Books (sixth), 109, 113
International Monetary Fund (IMF), 12, 50, 68, 110, 155
Irele, Abiola, Professor, 20
Ismail, Mohamed, of Garce, 21
Italian language, 35
Ituīka ceremony, 88
Ivory Coast, 64, 155

Jackson, Jesse, 112
James, C.L.R, 103, 129, 145, 148; *The Black Jacobins*, 142
Japan, 55, 121
Jara, Victor, 147
Journal of African Marxists, 70
Joyce, James, 6, 102–3, 105; *A Portrait of the Artist as a Young Man*, 102

Kabarega, 171
Kamīrīīthū Community and Cultural Centre, Limuru, Kenya, 93; open-air theatre burnt down (1982), 45, 72, 93, 175
Kamīrīīthū, Limuru, Kenya, 160
Kamenjū, Grant, 7, 8
Kamītī Maximum Security Prison, 102, 106, 157, 160
Kanyegenyūri, politically-conscious song, 44, 89
Kenya, 64, 71, 85–6, 90–2, 97, 98, 109, 119, 133, 155; cultural renaissance, 89; cultural repression, 85–6; neo-colonialist state, 71, 86; politics of culture, 88; rebirth of national literature, 94; theatre, 92–3
Kenya Land Freedom Army (see Mau Mau)
Kenya National Theatre, 92–3
Kenyatta, Jomo, 71, 103, 138, 151, 167, 168, 170, 173
Kenyatta University College, 72, 93

Index

Kettle, Arnold, Professor, 9
Kīmathi, Dedan, leader of KLFA (Mau Mau), 97–8, 100, 138, 147, 171
Kim Chi Ha, 13
Kipling, Rudyard, 4, 137; poem 'If', 137–8
Kiswahili, xiv, 11, 23, 26, 35, 38, 40–1, 156, 170; proposed as language for the world, 41; unifying language of culture and commerce in East Africa, 161
Kitur, Tirop arap, 109
Korea, North, 112
Korea, South, 51, 119
Kuene, Mazisi, 150

labour: black labour and white-owned capital, 62; struggle among humans for control of production, 96
Lamming, George, 6, 7, 65, 103; *In the Castle of My Skin*, 4, 5, 6, 65; *Season of Adventure*, 6; *The Pleasures of Exile*, 6
Laye, Camara: *The African Child*, 61
Leeds University, 2, 7, 107; Commonwealth Literature Conference (1964), 7; *Union News*, students' newspaper, 9
Lehane, Paul, 145
Lenin, V.I.: *Imperialism, The Highest Stage of Capitalism*, 6
Livingstone, David, 31
Lonnrot, Elias: *Kalevala*, 22
Lugard, Lord, 32
Lu Hsun, 13
Lumumba, Patrice, 66
Luther, Martin, 22

Maasai, 171
Maina wa Kīnyattī, 72, 98–9, 100–1; ed. *Thunder From the Mountains: Mau Mau Patriotic Songs*, 72, 100; *Mau Mau: The Highest Peak of Resistance*, 100; rescued KLFA papers, 99–100
Maji Maji armed struggle, Tanganyika (1905), 165, 171
Makerere University (College), Uganda, 5, 7, 8, 93, 103, 106, 164–5, 166, 168
Makhoere, Caesarina Kona, 104
Malawi, 64, 155, 164
Mali, 64, 66
Mandela, Nelson, xiv, 13, 146–151; infinite capacity of human spirit to resist and conquer, 147
Mandela, Winnie, 146
Mann, Thomas, 13

Mansfield, Katherine, 102, 105
Maori language, 40
Mapanje, Jack, 104, 104n
Marierid, Lyn, Welsh Language Society, 36
Marquez, Gabriel Garcia: *The Autumn of the Patriarch*, 71
Marx, Karl, xvi, 67–8, 148; *The Communist Manifesto*, 68
Mas'udi, al: *The Meadows of Gold and the Mines of Gems*, 172
Mau Mau (Kenya Land Freedom Army, KLFA), 2, 69, 72, 73, 89, 138, 151, 160, 171; papers rescued by Maina wa Kīnyattī, 99–100; struggle against British colonialism, 60, 97–8, 99–100; writers jailed or killed, 45
Mazrui, Al Amin, 72, 93, 103, 104; *Cry for Justice*, 93; *Kilio cha Haki*, 45
Mbarak Ibn Rashid, 171
Melville, Herman, 13; *Moby Dick*, 103
Milton, John, 22, 38; *Paradise Lost*, 14, 161
Miriyamu, Mozambique, 149
MNR (Renamo), Mozambique, 79, 80, 81
Mofolo, Thomas, 150
Mohamed, Bala, 70
Moi, Daniel arap, 71, 105, 151, 156, 159, 169
Moi-KANU regime, Kenya, 45, 103, 105, 173
Monsarrat, Nicholas, 35, 140
Morning Star, newspaper: article on decline of Welsh language, 36
Mozambique, 64, 69, 78–9, 99, 100, 156
Mphahlele, Ezekiel, 8, 150
Mūgo, Mīcere, 72
Mūngai, Samuel, 109
Museveni, Yoweri, 166, 169, 173
Mussolini, Benito, 123
Mūthīrīgū: politically-conscious song/dance, 44, 89
Mwakawa, 171
Mwakenya: Draft Minimum Programme (1987), 173
Mwanga, 171
Mwinyi, Ali Hassan, 173

Nabudere, Dan, 70
Naipaul, V.S., 102
Nairobi declaration on unity of East Africa, 166, 174
Nairobi University, 8, 93; travelling theatre, 93

Namibia, 86, 116
Nazareth, Peter, 7
Nazi Germany, 121, 123
Nduthu, Karīmi, 109
Negritude, African writers' movement, 105
Nehanda, Mbuya, 147
neo-colonialism, 37, 44, 106; African writers face to face with, 70–1; ante-neo-colonial guerrilla movements, 74, 111; as last stage of imperialism (Nkrumah), 53, 57; Kenya a good example, 71; seventies reveal neo-colonial character of many African countries, 69
Neruda, Pablo, 7
Ngūgī wa Mīrīi, 45, 72, 105; *Ngaahika Ndeenda* (*I Will Marry When I Want*), co-authored with Ngūgī wa Thiong'o, 174
Ngūgī wa Thiong'o: as translator, 41; decision to write in Gīkūyū, 9, 94; sense of own exile from Kenya, 155; WORKS: *Barrel of a Pen*, 93; *The Black Hermit*, 45, 165; *Decolonising the Mind*, 10, 30, 32, 84n, 93; *Detained: A Writer's Prison Diary*, 93, 102; *Devil on the Cross* (*Caitaani Mūtharabinī*), 94, 102, 106, 157; *A Grain of Wheat*, 2, 3, 5, 9, 107; *The Impact of Donors and Development Assistance on the Recipient Cultures*, 154–5; *Kariūki*, 155; *Maitū Njugīra*, 45, 174; *Matigari*, 106, 155, 157, 159, 161, 163, 175; *Memories of Childhood*, 2; *Mother, Sing for Me*, 93; *Ngaahika Ndeenda* (I Will Marry When I Want), co-authored with Ngūgī wa Mīrīi, 93, 174; *Petals of Blood*, 103; *The River Between*, 4, 5, 163, 165; *The Trial of Dedan Kīmathi*, 92–3; *Weep Not, Child*, 4, 5, 165
Nicaragua: Contras, 49; under Somoza, 51
Nigeria, 2, 60, 66
Nkosi, Lewis: *Home and Exile*, 106
Nkosi Sikelele Africa (*God Bless Africa*), 150
Nkrumah, Kwame, 53, 57, 147; *Towards Colonial Freedom*, 61
Nyerere, Julius, 166, 167–8, 173: *Ujamaa: the basis of African socialism*, 63
Nzongola-Ntalaja, 70

Obote, Apollo Milton, 167, 168, 169, 170, 173
Odessey, The, 22
Okot p'Bitek: *Song of Lawino*, 67
oral tradition, orature in African literature, 18, 21, 22, 88
Ousmane, Sembene, 13, 38; *God's Bits of Wood*, 61
Owen, Wilfrid, 6
Oxford English Dictionary, 23
Oyugi, Edward, 72

Padmore, George, 145
Palme, Olof, 155
Pan-African Congress, 150
Pan-Africanism, 74, 113
Penpoint literary journal, 165
petty-bourgeoisie, 63; inherited management of ex-colonies, 51–2
Philippines, The, 119; under Marcos, 51
Portugal, 48
Portuguese language, 8, 32, 35, 37, 40–1; arrival in Third World, 31, 32; as language of new African literature, 107
prison 'graduates', 104
Pushkin, Alexander, 13, 22

Rabelais, François, 22
Racism, 118–9; five interlinked features, 117; in Britain, 137–9
Ravenscroft, Arthur, Professor, 2, 4, 7, 9, 10; lecture at Leeds University (1990), xiii
Reagan, Ronald, ex-President of USA, 37
Rhodesian Front, 64
Rider Haggard, Sir Henry, 35, 140
Robeson, Paul, 4, 147
Rodney, Walter, 70, 98, 100, 103; *How Europe Underdeveloped Africa*, 166
Ruark, Robert, 35
Russian language, 40
Russian revolution (1917), 48, 111

Saadawi, Nawal el, 104
Sartre, Jean-Paul, 14
Schiller, Friedrich von, 13, 22
Seacole, Mary, 145
Senegal, 64
Senghor, Léopold Sédar, 105
Shaka, King of the Zulus, 149
Shakespeare, William, 6, 13, 22, 38, 137; *King Lear*, 14; *Julius Caesar*, 14; *The Tempest*, 15, 19

Index

Sharpeville, 17, 60, 147, 149
Shaw, George Bernard, 38
Shelley, Percy Bysshe, 38
Shivji, Issa: *The Silent Class Struggle: The Dar Debate on Imperialism, Nationality and Class*, 166
Sholokhov, Mikhail, 38
Shona language, 38, 156
Sierra Leone, 66
slave trade and slavery, 28, 54, 123, 129
Smith, Adam, 148
Smith, Ian, 64
Somali language, 38
South Africa, 55, 100, 111, 116, 119, 120–1, 124, 143, 148, 151; apartheid, 60, 81, 110, 120–1, 143; Boer racist regime, 65; last of colonial Africa, 107; liberation of SA key to social liberation of continent, 76–7
South African Communist Party, 150
Soweto, 17, 80, 147, 149
Soyinka, Wole, 7, 13; *A Dance of the Forests*, 61; first African Nobel prizewinner for literature, 104
Spain, 48
Spanish language, 11, 40
Spenser, Edmund, 6, 22
Stevenson, Robert Louis, 136; *Treasure Island*, 136–7
Sudan, 66, 69

Tagore, Rabindranath, 7
Tanganyika, 164, 165, 166
Tanzania, 2, 64, 150, 155, 162–8, 170–3
Third World, 53, 124; four main areas and four stages in development, 55; literatures have much to learn from each other, 56; racism between West and Third World, 118–9
Thuku, Harry, 89
Tlali, Miriam, 150
Tolstoy, Leo, 13
Toussaint L'Overture, 147
Transition, literary journal, 165
Turner, Nat, 147

Uganda, 2, 64, 66, 69, 162–4, 166–9, 167–170, 170–6
Umkhonto we Sizwe (the Spear of the Nation), 17
UNESCO, 52

UNITA, Angola, 49, 79, 81
United Nations Security Council, xvi; offical languages, 38
United States of America, 112, 124, 143, 149; capitalism into imperialism into neo-colonial policies, 47, 51; controls media of Third World with West, 52–3; invasion of Grenada, 49; leader of imperialism, 47; military bases round Africa, 68; role in Lumumba/Mobutu conflict, Zaire, 66; support for repressive regimes, 51

Vieira, José Luandino, 38
Victoria, Queen, 37
Vietnam, 112
Vilikazi, B.H., 150

Walker, Alice, 13
Walsh, William, Professor, 8; launch of *Journal of Commonwealth Literature*, 8
Wangūi wa Goro, 41
Washington, Booker T: *Up from Slavery*; 43
Wästberg, Per, 155; *Eldens Skugga (The Shadows of Fire), Bergets Kalla (Source of the Mountain)*, 155
Wedderburn, Robert, 145
Whitman, Walt, 14
Williams, Eric, 129, 148; *Capitalism and Slavery*, 142
Wolof language, 38
World Bank, 12, 50, 68, 110
Wright, Richard, 7, 13
writers in exile from Africa, 105

Yale University, 154–5; Conference: Tradition and Transition in African Letters (April 1990), 24; *Journal of Criticism*, xiii, 156
Yeats, William Butler, 5
Yoruba language, 156

Zaire, 2, 64, 66, 69; Mobutu regime, 66
Zambia, 135, 164
Zimbabwe, 64, 69, 99, 100, 150, 155, 164
Zirimu, Pio, 7, 8
Zirimu, Van, 8
Zulu language, 156